Wedding Songs for Vocal Duet

Arranged by Donald Sosin

CONTENTS

Cherry Lane Music Company
Director of Publications/Project Editor: Mark Phillips

ISBN 1-57560-762-X

Visit our website at www.cherrylane.com

Amazing Grace

Words by John Newton
From *A Collection of Sacred Ballads*

Traditional American Melody
From Carrell and Clayton's *Virginia Harmony*

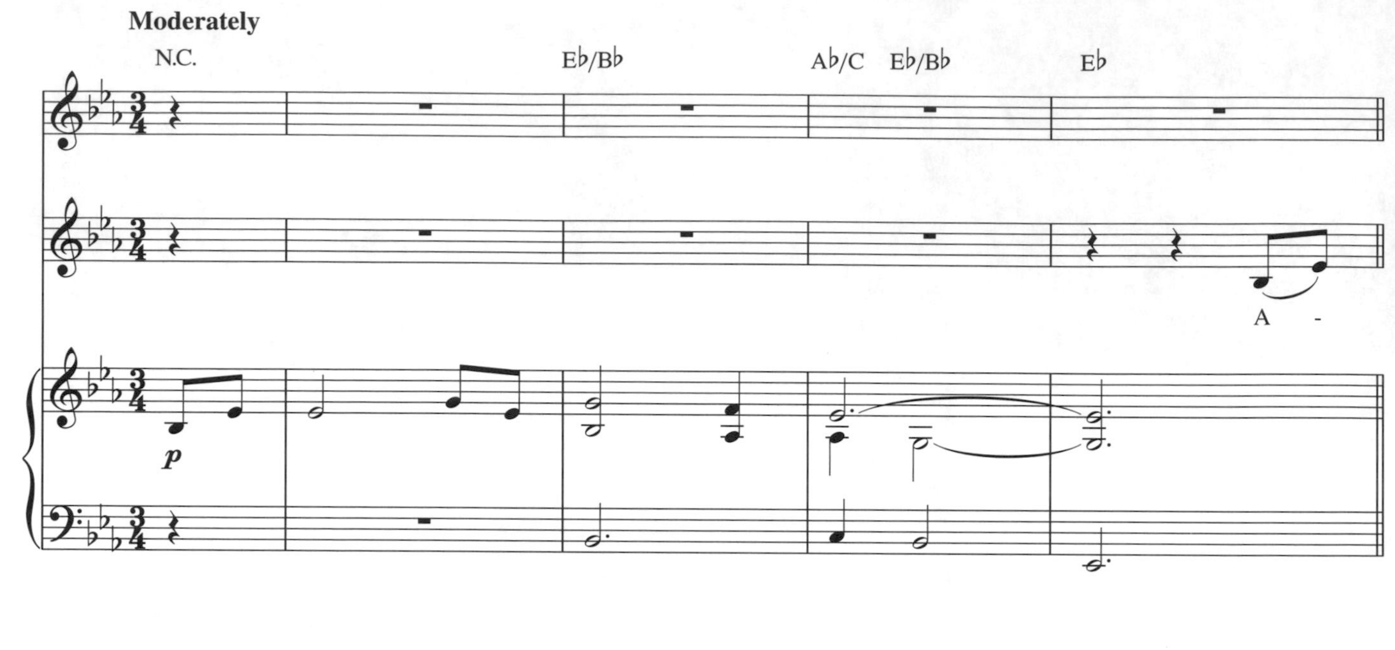

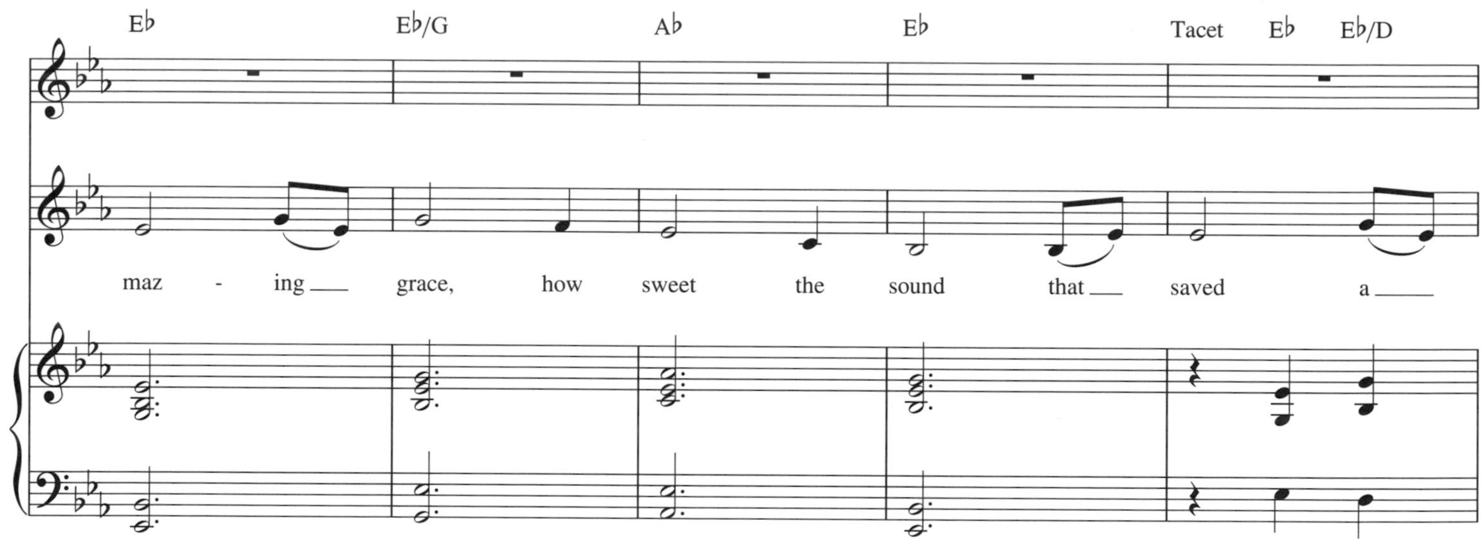

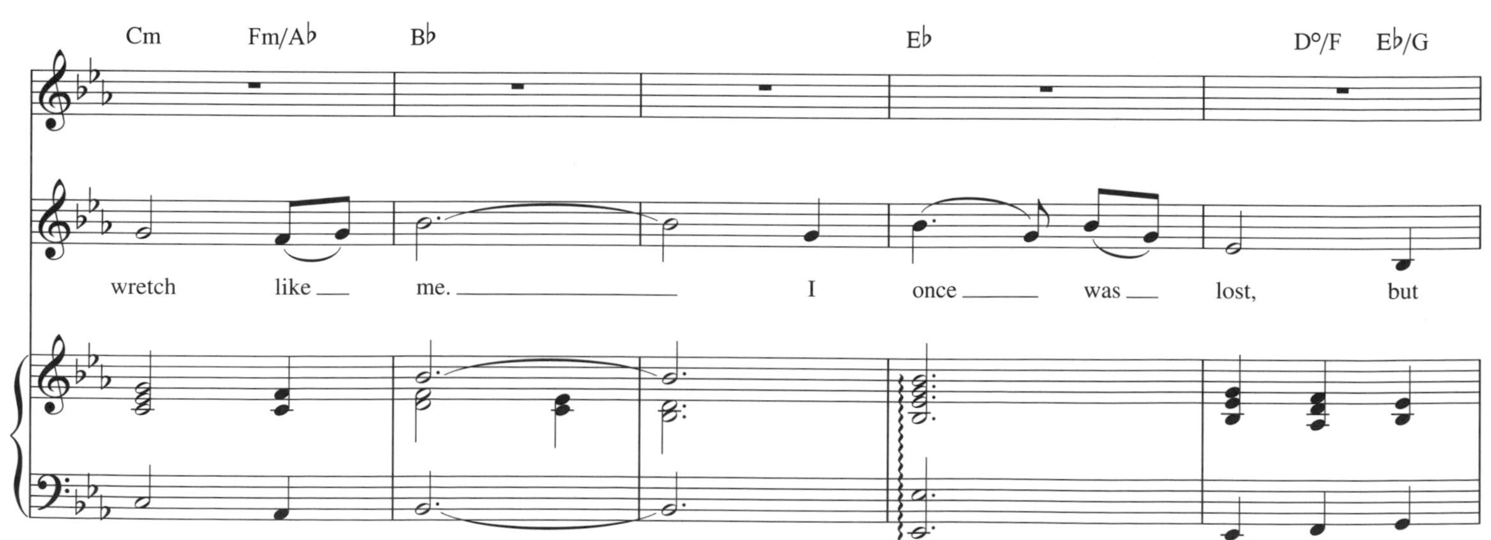

A♭
E♭
E♭/B♭
A♭maj7
B♭
A♭/E♭
now am found, was blind but now I see.
E♭
A♭
D♭
A♭
'Twas grace that taught my heart to fear, and
that taught my heart to fear, and
E♭/G
Fm
E♭
A♭
grace my fears re - lieved. How
grace my fears re - lieved. How

Db
Ab
pre - cious did that grace ap - pear the
pre - cious did that grace ap - pear the

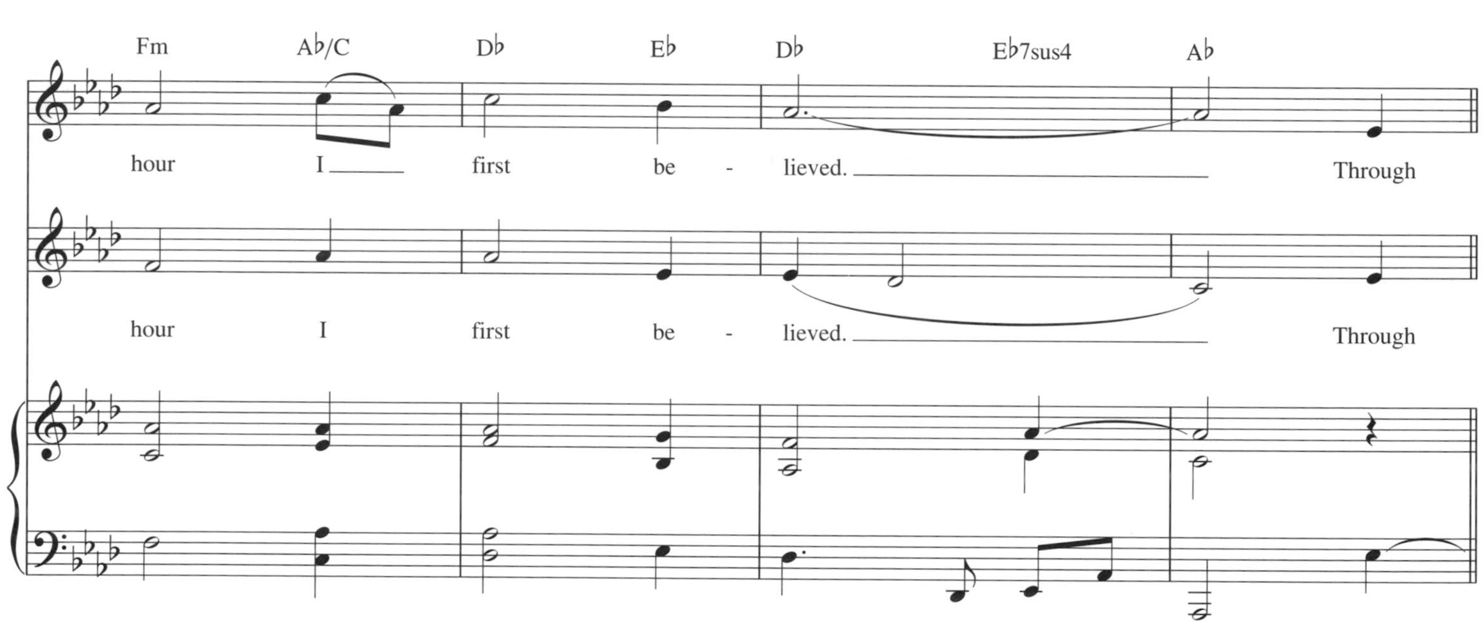
Fm
Ab/C
Db
Eb
Db
Eb7sus4
Ab
hour I first be - lieved. Through
hour I first be - lieved. Through

Gospel style
Ab
Dbadd2
Db/Ab
Ab
Eb
man - y dan - gers, toils, and snares, I
man - y dan - gers, toils, and snares, I
f

A♭
Fm/G
Fm
Fm7add4
E♭
have al - read - y come. 'Tis
have al - read - y come. 'Tis
A♭
B♭m7
A♭/C
D♭
A♭
grace that brought me safe this far and
grace that brought me safe this far and
A♭/E♭
E♭
D♭
A♭
grace will lead me home.
grace will lead me home.

Ave Maria

By Charles Gounod

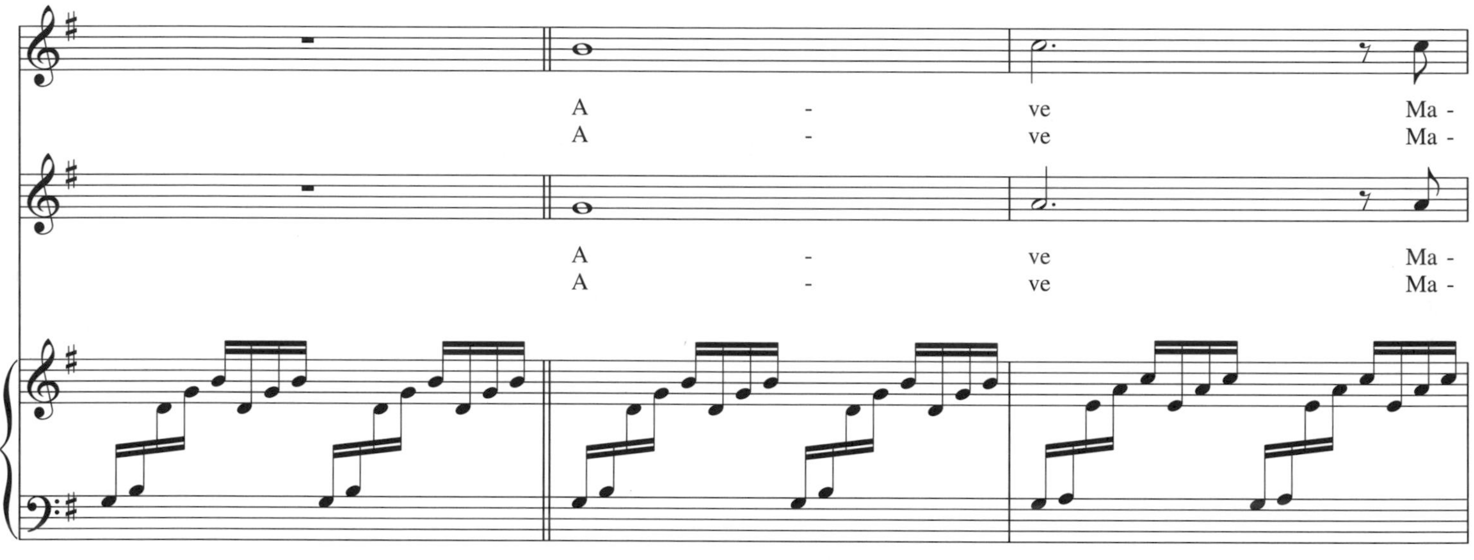

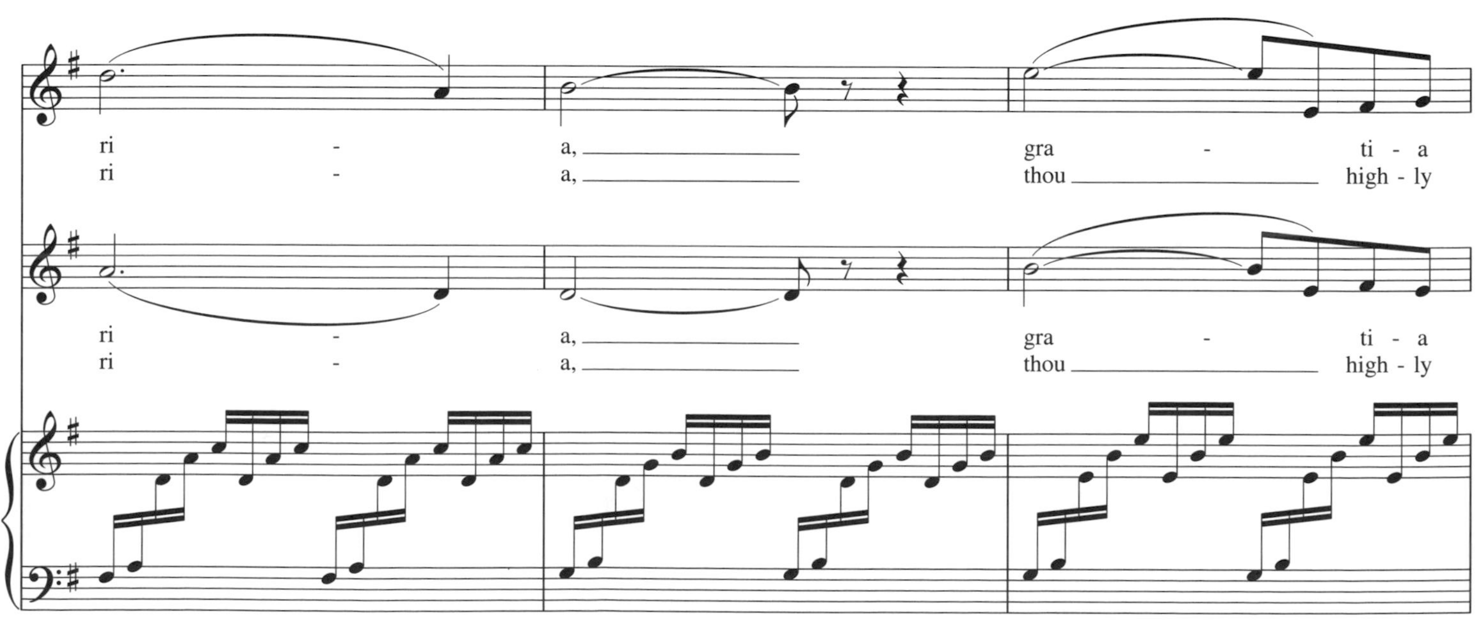

ple - na,
fa - vored,
Do - mi - nus
God is
te - cum,
with thee.
ple - na,
fa - vored,
Do - mi - nus
God is
te - cum,
with thee.
be - ne - dic - ta tu in
Bless - ed, bless - ed art thou, art
be - ne - dic - ta tu in
Bless - ed, bless - ed art thou, art
mu - li - e - ri - bus et be - ne -
thou a - bove all wom - en, bless - ed be thine
mu - li - e - ri - bus et be - ne -
thou a - bove all wom - en, bless - ed be thine

dic - tus fruc - tus ven - tris
off - spring, bless - ed be thy son, the Son of
dic - tus fruc - tus ven - tris
off - spring, bless - ed be thy son, the Son of

tu - i Je - sus. Sanc - ta Ma -
God, the Lord most high! Bless - ed Ma -
tu - i Je - sus. Sanc - ta Ma -
God, the Lord most high! Bless - ed Ma -

ri - a, sanc - ta Ma - ri - a, Ma -
ri - a! Bless - ed Ma - ri - a! Ma -
ri - a, sanc - ta Ma - ri - a, Ma -
ri - a! Bless - ed Ma - ri - a! Ma -

ri - a, o - ra pro no - bis,
ri - a! Pray, oh, pray, for us,
ri - a, o - ra pro no - bis,
ri - a! Pray, oh, pray, for us,
no - bis pec - ca - to - ri - bus,
for us wretch - ed sin - ners,
no - bis pec - ca - to - ri - bus,
for us wretch - ed sin - ners,
cresc.
nunc et in ho - ra
now and when the hour
nunc et in ho - ra in
now and when the hour of our
f

in ho - ra mor - tis nos - trae,
of our death o'er - takes us,
ho - ra mor - tis nos - trae,
death, our death o'er - takes us,

A - men!
A - men!
A - men!
A - men!
dim.
mp

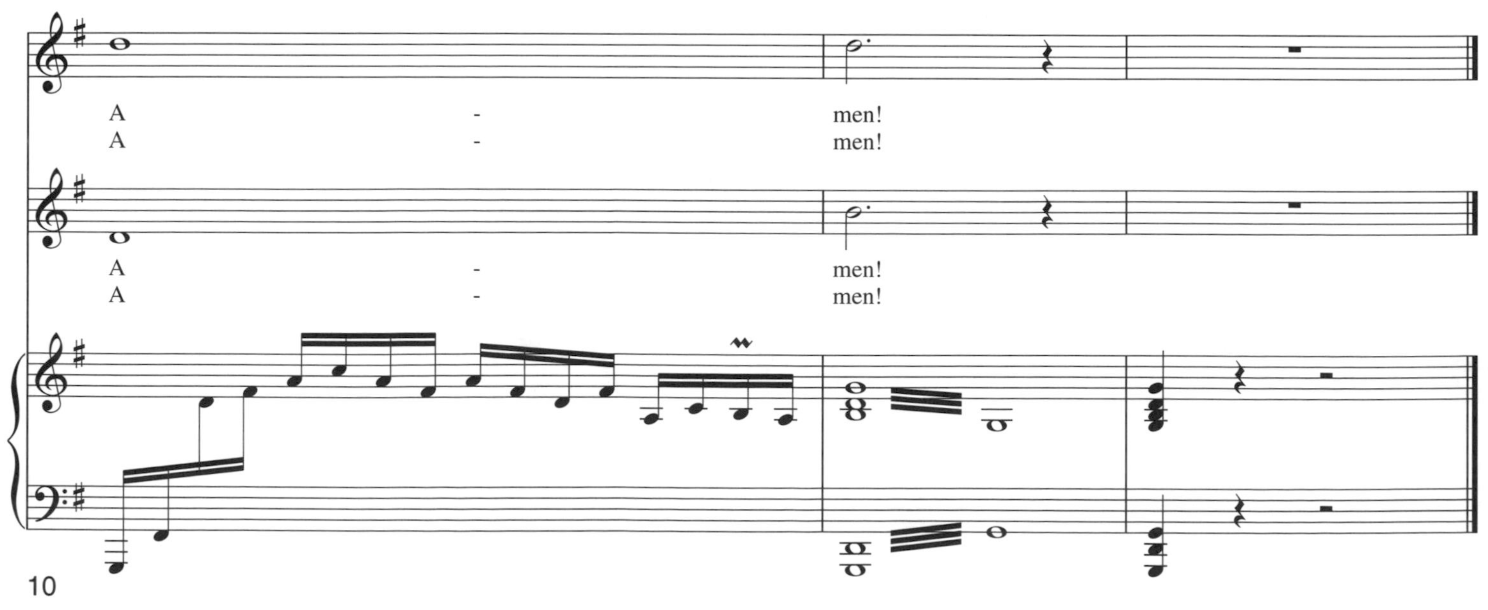
A - men!
A - men!
A - men!
A - men!

Ave Maria

By Franz Schubert

na. A - ve! A - ve! Do - mi - nus, Do - mi - nus te - cum. Be - ne -
na. A - ve! A - ve! Do - mi - nus te - cum.

dic - ta tu in mu - li - e - ri - bus et be - ne - dic - tus, et
Be - ne - dic - ta tu in mu - li - e - ri - bus, be - ne - dic - tus, et

be - ne - dic - tus fruc - tus ven - tris, ven - tris tu - i Je - sus.
be - ne - di - ctus fruc - tus ven - tris, ven - tris tu - i Je - sus.

A - ve Ma - ri - a!
A - ve Ma - ri - a!
A - ve Ma - ri -
a! Ma - ter De - i, O - ra pro no - bis pec - ca -
Ma - ri - a, Ma - ter De - i, O - ra pro

to - ri - bus, O - ra o - ra _ pro no - bis, O - ra, o - ra _ pro no -
no - bis, O - ra pro no - bis, O - ra, pro no -
bis pec - ca - to - ri - bus, nunc, et in ho - ra _ mor - tis, in
bis pec - ca - to - ri - bus, nunc, et in ho - ra mor - tis, in
ho - ra mor - tis no - strae, in ho - ra mor - tis, mor - tis no - strae, in
ho - ra mor - tis no - strae, in ho - ra mor - tis, mor - tis no - strae, in

ho - ra mor - tis no - strae.
A - ve Ma - ri -
ho - ra mor - tis no - strae.
A - ve Ma - ri -
a!
a!
dim.
p

Bist du bei mir
(Be Thou with Me)

By Johann Sebastian Bach

Be thou with me, my joy and
Bist du bei mir, geh' ich mit
Be thou with me, my joy and
Bist du bei mir, geh' ich mit
glad - ness. In deep re - pose my soul shall
Freu - den. Zum Ster - ben und zu mei - ner
glad - ness. In deep re - pose my soul shall
Freu - den. Zum Ster - ben und zu mei - ner
rest, my soul shall rest in deep re - pose.
Ruh', zum Ster - ben und zu mei - ner Ruh'.
rest, my soul shall rest in deep re - pose.
Ruh', zum Ster - ben und zu mei - ner Ruh'.

My heart is glad when thou art
Ach, wie ver - gnüst wär' so mein
My heart is glad when thou art
Ach, wie ver - gnüst wär' so mein

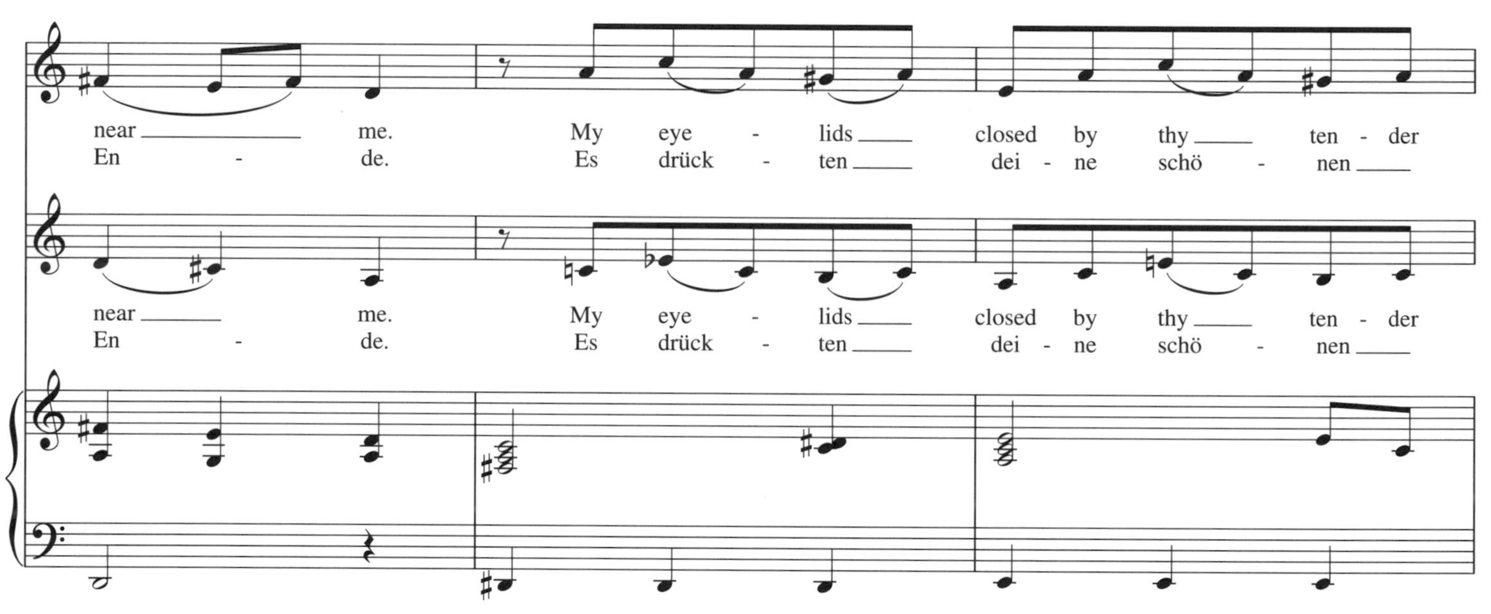
near me. My eye - lids closed by thy ten - der
En - de. Es drück - ten dei - ne schö - nen
near me. My eye - lids closed by thy ten - der
En - de. Es drück - ten dei - ne schö - nen

hands, my eyes with love will rest on thee.
Hän - de mir die ge - treu - en Au - gen zu.
hands, my eyes with love will rest on thee.
Hän - de mir die ge - treu - en Au - gen zu.

My heart is glad when thou art
Ach, wie ver - gnüst wär' so mein
My heart is glad when thou art
Ach, wie ver - gnüst wär' so mein
near me. My eye - lids closed by thy ten - der
En - de. Es drück - ten dei - ne schö - nen
near me.
En - de.
hands, my eyes with love will rest on thee.
Hän - de mir die ge - treu - en Au - gen zu.
My eyes with love will rest on thee.
mir die ge - treu - en Au - gen zu.

Be thou with me, my joy and
Bist du bei mir, geh' ich mit
Be thou with me, my joy and
Bist du bei mir, geh' ich mit

glad - ness. In deep re - pose my soul shall
Freu - den. Zum Ster - ben und zu mei - ner
glad - ness. In deep re - pose my soul shall
Freu - den. Zum Ster - ben und zu mei - ner

rest, my soul shall rest in deep re - pose.
Ruh', zum Ster - ben und zu mei - ner Ruh'.
rest, my soul shall rest in deep re - pose.
Ruh', zum Ster - ben und zu mei - ner Ruh'.

Butterfly Kisses

Words and Music by
Bob Carlisle and Randy Thomas

Dm7 C/E Gsus4/F G7sus4 G7 Dm7 Cadd2/E
drop to my knees by her bed at night, she talks to Je - sus and
One part wom - an, the oth - er part girl. To per - fume and make - up from
Stand - ing in the bride room just star - ing at her, she asked me what I'm think - ing, and I
drop to my knees by her bed at night, she talks to Je - sus and
One part wom - an, the oth - er part girl. To per - fume and make - up from
Stand - ing in the bride room just star - ing at her, she asked me what I'm think - ing, and I
Fsus2 G7sus4 G7 Fadd2/A Gsus2/B Cadd2
I close my eyes, and I thank God for all of the joy in my
rib - bons and curls. Try - ing her wings out in a great big
said, "I'm not sure. I just feel like I'm los - ing my ba - by
I close my eyes, and I thank God for all of the joy in my
rib - bons and curls. Try - ing her wings out in a great big
said, "I'm not sure. I just feel like I'm los - ing my ba - by
Fsus2/A G7sus4 Csus4/2 C
life. Oh, but most of all for but - ter - fly kiss - es af - ter
world. But I re - mem - ber but - ter - fly kiss - es af - ter
girl." Then she leaned o - ver, gave me but - ter - fly kiss - es with her
life. Oh, but most of all for but - ter - fly kiss - es af - ter
world. But I re - mem - ber but - ter - fly kiss - es af - ter
girl." Then she leaned o - ver, gave me but - ter - fly kiss - es with her
mf

Csus4/2 C C6sus4/2 C G/C
bed - time pray'r, stick - in' lit - tle white flow - ers all up in her
bed - time pray'r, stick - in' lit - tle white flow - ers all up in her
ma - ma there, stick - in' lit - tle white flow - ers all up in her
bed - time pray'r, stick - in' lit - tle white flow - ers all up in her
bed - time pray'r, stick - in' lit - tle white flow - ers all up in her
ma - ma there, stick - in' lit - tle white flow - ers all up in her
Am Gsus4/2 G Fadd2
hair. "Walk be - side the po - ny, Dad - dy; it's
hair. "You know how much I love you, Dad - dy, but if
hair. "Walk me down the ai - sle, Dad - dy; it's
hair.
hair.
hair.
Csus2/E Fadd2 Csus2/E C/E
my first ride. I know the cake looks fun - ny, Dad - dy, but I sure tried."
you don't mind, I'm on - ly go'n' to kiss you on the cheek this time."
just a - bout time. Does my wed-ding gown look pret - ty, Dad - dy? Dad-dy, don't cry."
Oh, with
Oh, with

Fsus2/A
Gsus2/B
C
D7sus4
D7
all that I've done wrong, I must have done some - thing right to de - serve a hug ev - 'ry morn - ing and but - ter - fly kiss - es at night.
her love
her love
all that I've done wrong, I must have done some - thing right.
rit.
To Coda
F
G7sus4
1.
Csus4/2
C
And but - ter - fly kiss - es at night.
a tempo
mp
2.
Dm/C
G/A
F/G
mf

Csus4/2
C
E♭add2
Dm7add4
All the pre - cious time.
Like the
All the pre - cious time.
Dm/C
C
Dm/C
C
E♭add2
Dm7add4
wind, the years go by.
Pre-cious but - ter - fly,
Pre-cious but - ter - fly,
D.S. al Coda
Coda
F/A
Dm7
G7
G7sus4
G
spread your wings and fly.
but - ter - fly kiss - es.
I could-n't
spread your wings and fly.
but - ter - fly kiss - es.

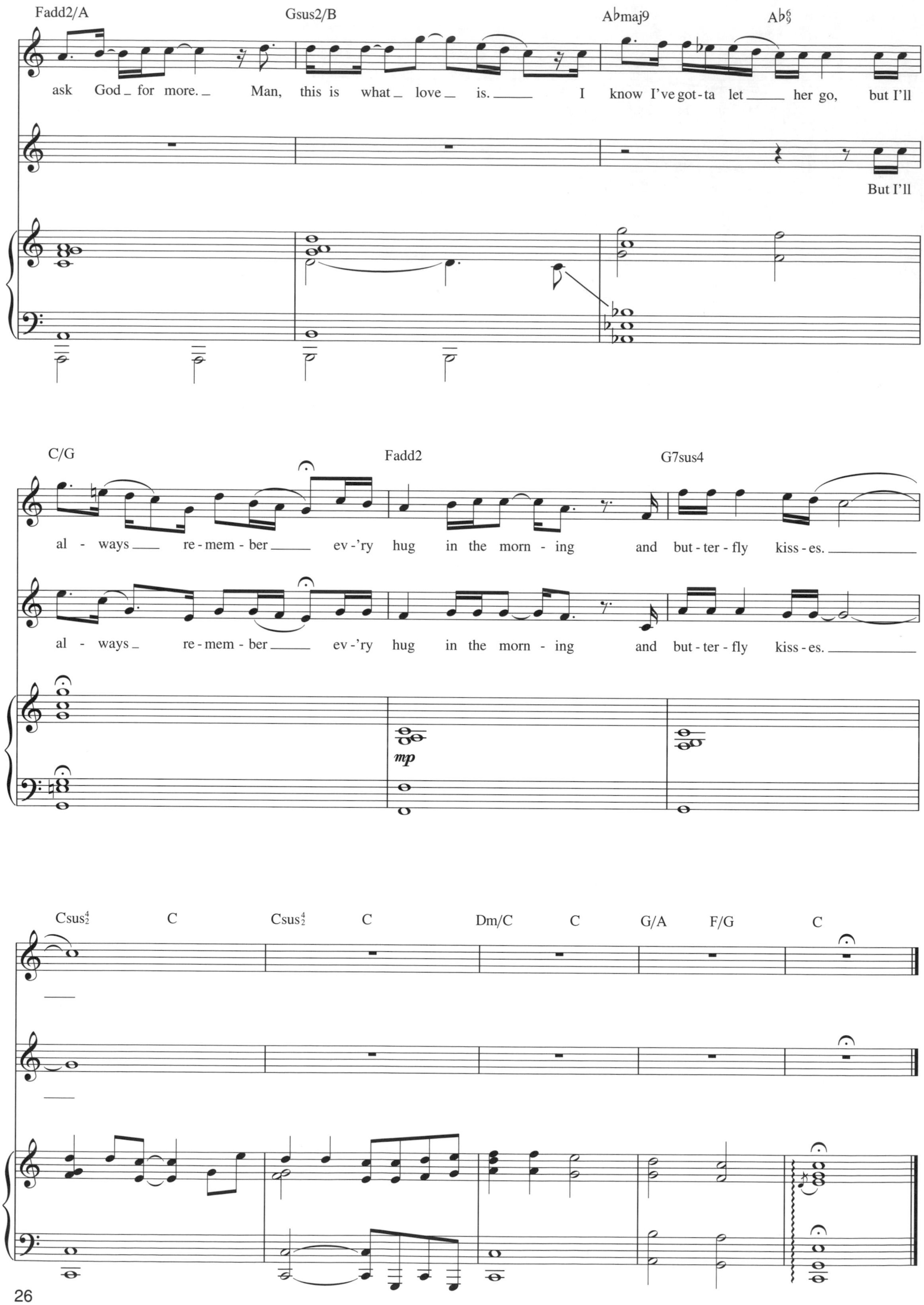

Fadd2/A Gsus2/B A♭maj9 A♭6/9

ask God for more. Man, this is what love is. I know I've got-ta let her go, but I'll

But I'll

C/G Fadd2 G7sus4

al - ways re-mem-ber ev-'ry hug in the morn - ing and but-ter-fly kiss-es.

al - ways re-mem-ber ev-'ry hug in the morn - ing and but-ter-fly kiss-es.

mp

Flower Duet

from LAKMÉ

By Leo Delibes

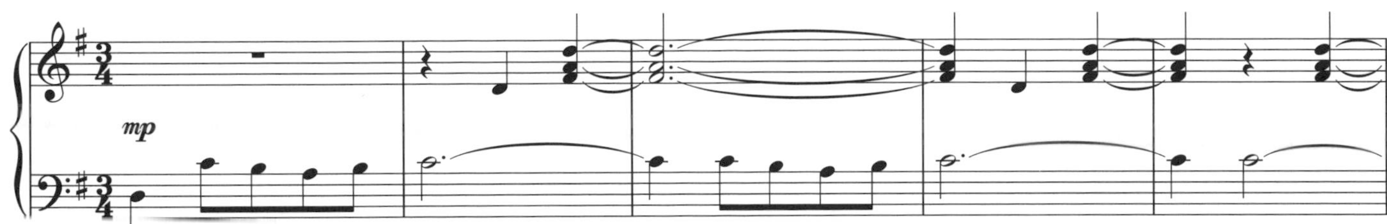

Rive en fleurs frais ma - tin, nous ap -
Sur la rive en fleurs, ri - ant au ma - tin, viens des -

pel - lent en - sem - ble. Ah! glis - sons
cen - dons en - sem - ble. Dou - ce - ment glis - sons,
mf

en sui - vant le cou - rant
de son flot char - mant, sui - vons le cou - rant
p
mf

fu - yant, dans l'on - de fré - mis -
fu - yant, dans l'on - de fré - mis -
san - te, d'u - ne main non-cha - lan -
san - te, d'u - ne main non-cha - lan -
p
te, ga - gnons le bord, où l'oi -
te, viens, ga - gnons le bord où la source dort,

seau chan - te, l'oi - seau, l'oi - seau chan - te. Dôme
et l'oi - seau, l'oi - seau chan - te. Sous le
rit.
a tempo
é - pais, blanc jas - min, nous ap - pel -
dôme é - pais, où le blanc jas - min. Ah! des - cen -
lent en - sem - ble!
dons en - sem - ble!
rit.

Follow Me

Words and Music by
John Denver

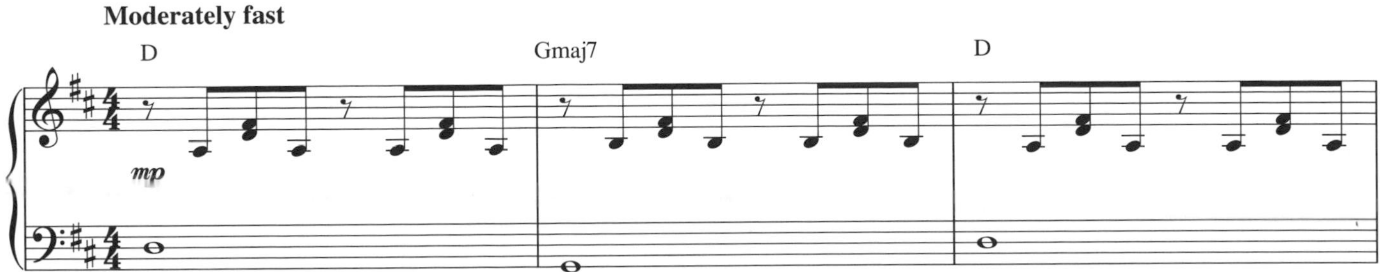
Moderately fast
D
Gmaj7
D
mp

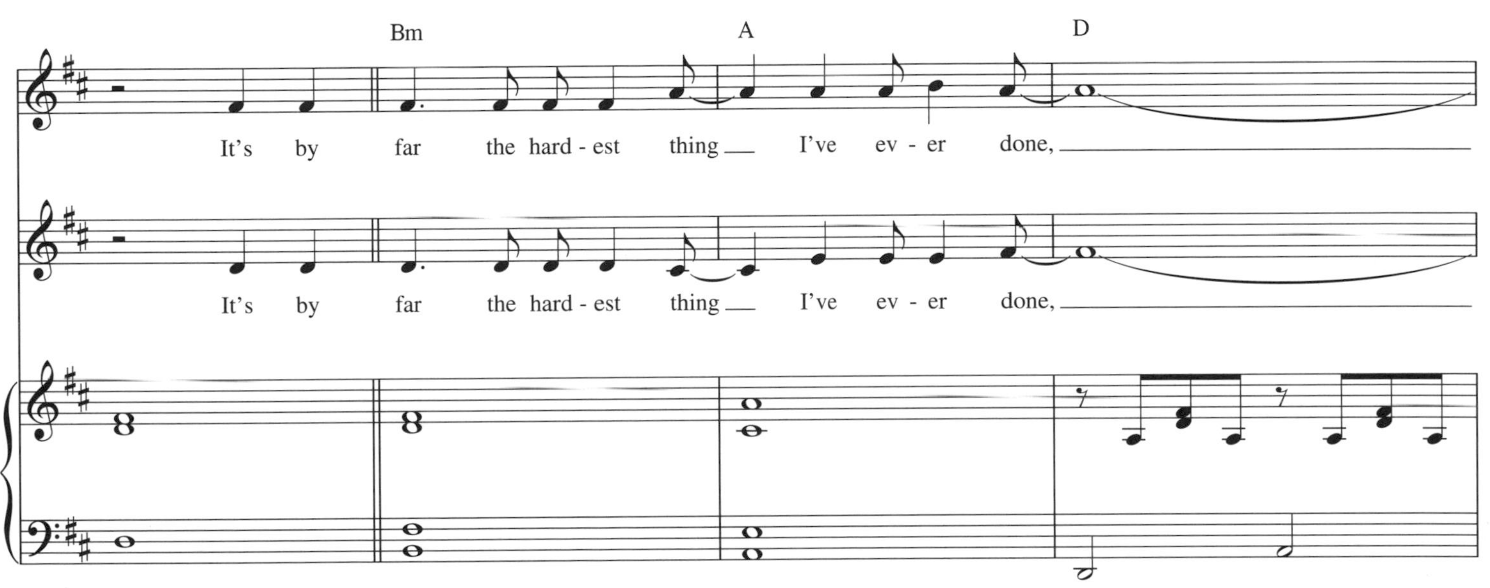
Bm
A
D
It's by far the hard - est thing ___ I've ev - er done, ___
It's by far the hard - est thing ___ I've ev - er done, ___

G
G/F♯
Em7
A
___ to be so in love with you and so a - lone. ___
___ to be so in love with you and so a - lone. ___

A7
D
Em7
D
Fol - low me where I go, what I do and who I know.
Fol - low me where I go, what I do and who I know.

G
D
Em7
A
Make it part of you to be a part of me.
Make it part of you to be a part of me.

To Coda
A7
D
Em7
D
3
Fol - low me up and down, all the way and all a - round.
Fol - low me up and down, all the way and all a - round.

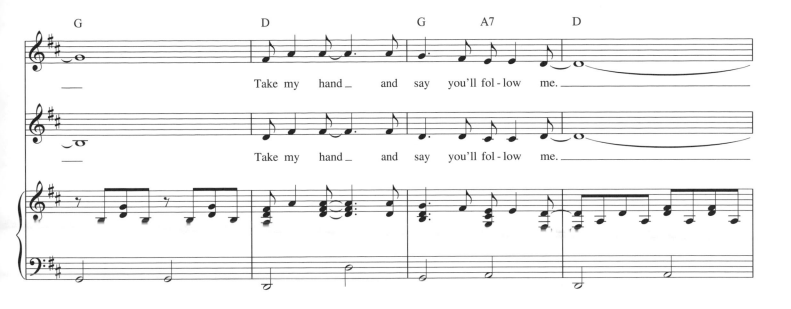

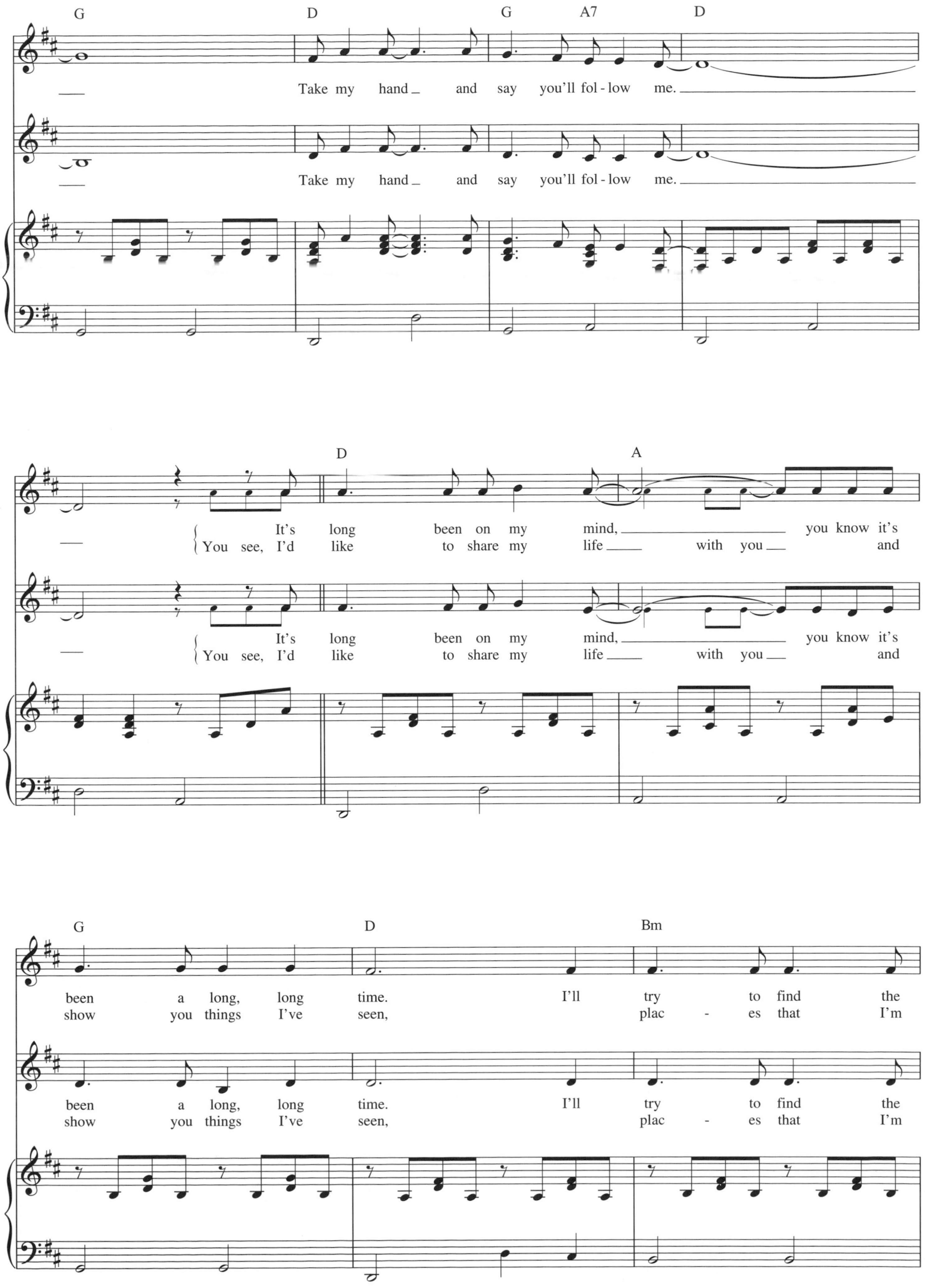

G D G A7 D

Take my hand and say you'll fol - low me.

Take my hand and say you'll fol - low me.

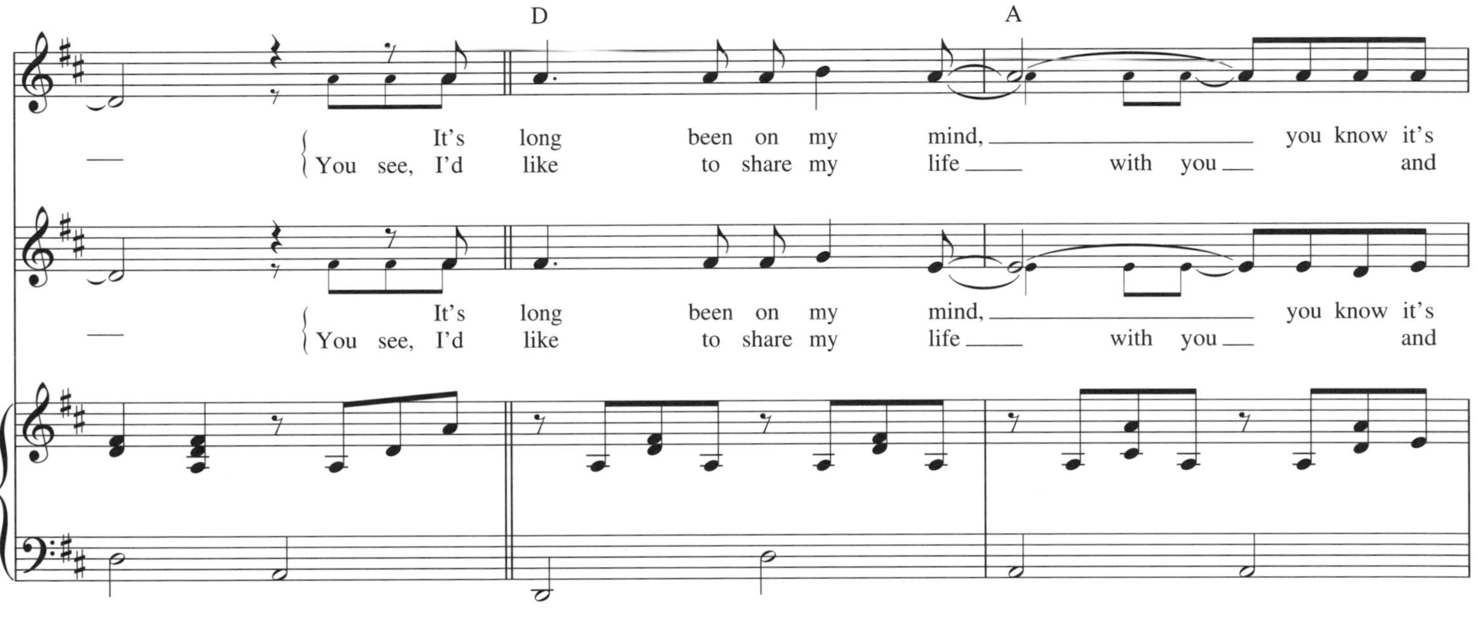
D
A
It's long been on my mind, you know it's
You see, I'd like to share my life with you and
It's long been on my mind, you know it's
You see, I'd like to share my life with you and

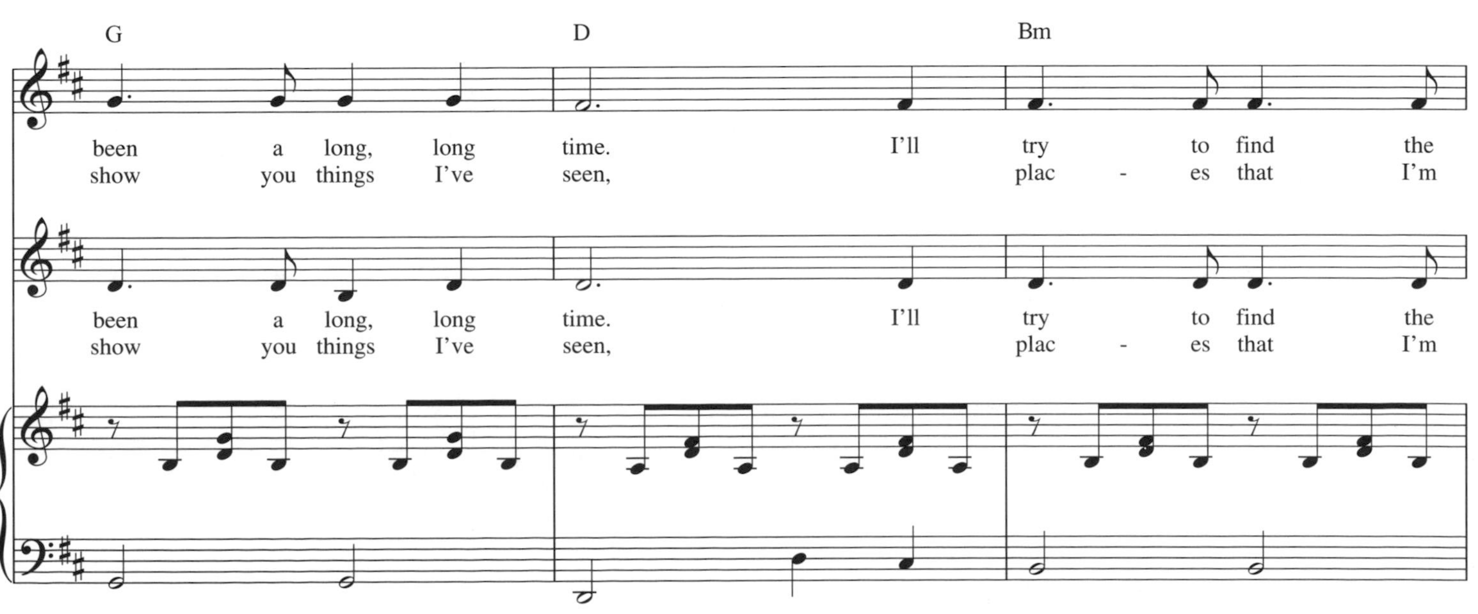
G
D
Bm
been a long, long time. I'll try to find the
show you things I've seen, plac - es that I'm
been a long, long time. I'll try to find the
show you things I've seen, plac - es that I'm

A
G
A
way that I can make you un - der - stand the
go - ing to, plac - es where I've been, to
way that I can make you un - der - stand the
go - ing to, plac - es where I've been, to

G
D
G
way I feel a - bout you and just how much I
have you there be - side me and nev - er be a -
way I feel a - bout you and just how much I
have you there be - side me and nev - er be a -

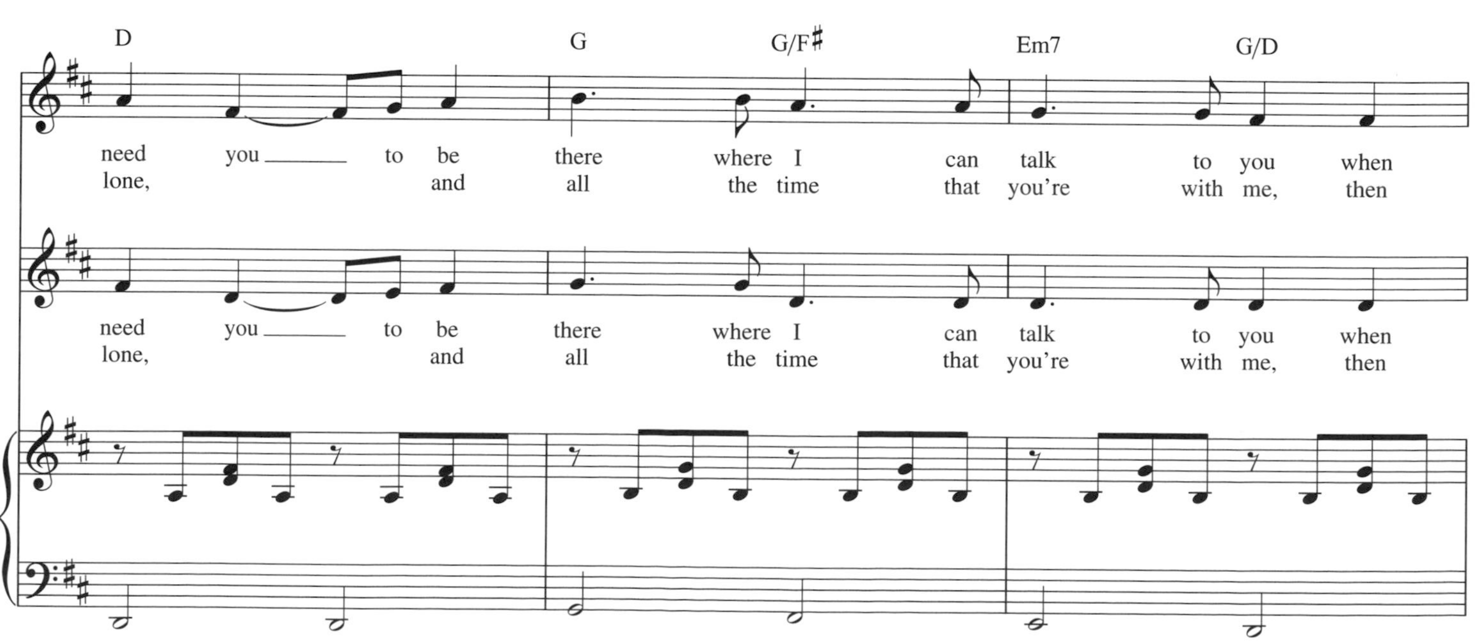

D
G
G/F♯
Em7
G/D
need you to be there where I can talk to you when
lone, and all the time that you're with me, then
need you to be there where I can talk to you when
lone, and all the time that you're with me, then

1.
2.
D.S. al Coda
G
A
A7
A7
there's no one else a - round.
we will be at home.
Fol - low me
Fol - low me
there's no one else a - round.
we will be at home.
Fol - low me
Fol - low me
Coda
D
G
D
way.
Take my hand and
way.
Take my hand and
G
A7
D
say you'll fol - low me.
say you'll fol - low me.

For Always

from the Motion Picture A.I. ARTIFICIAL INTELLIGENCE

Lyric by Cynthia Weil

Music by John Williams

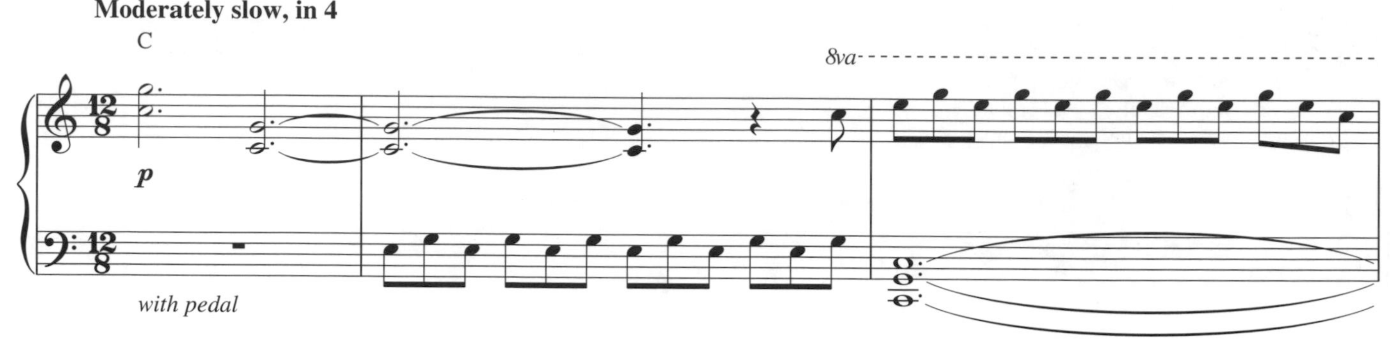

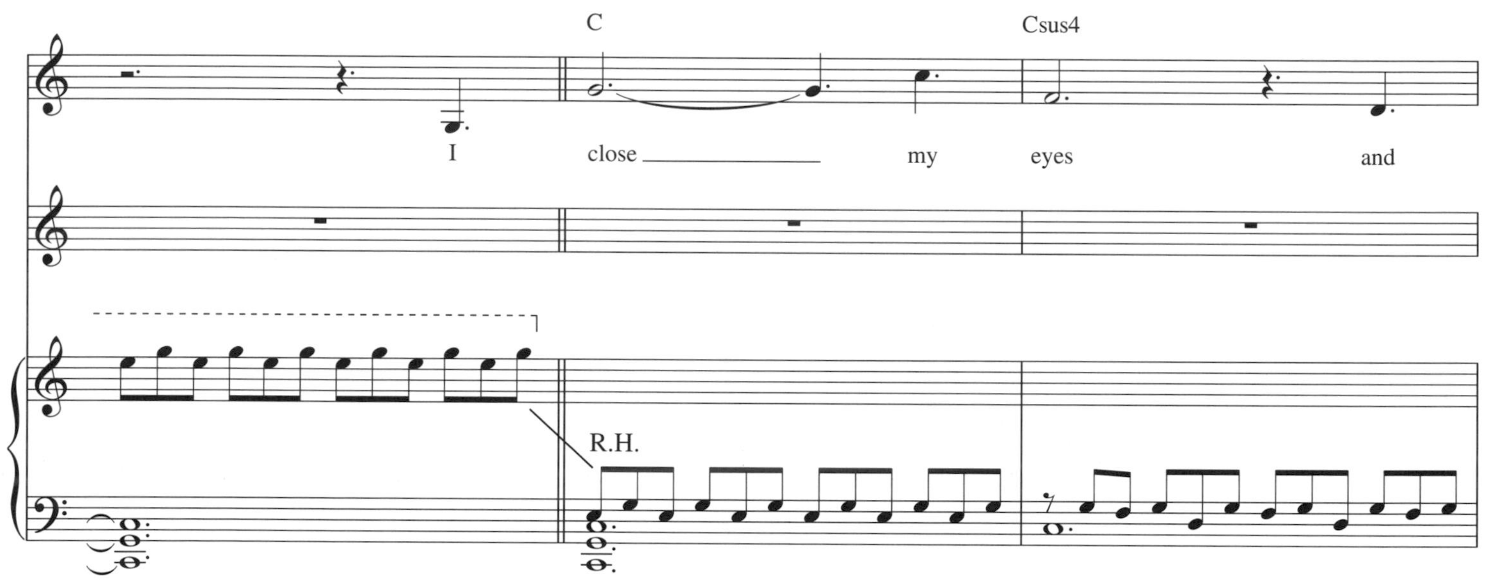

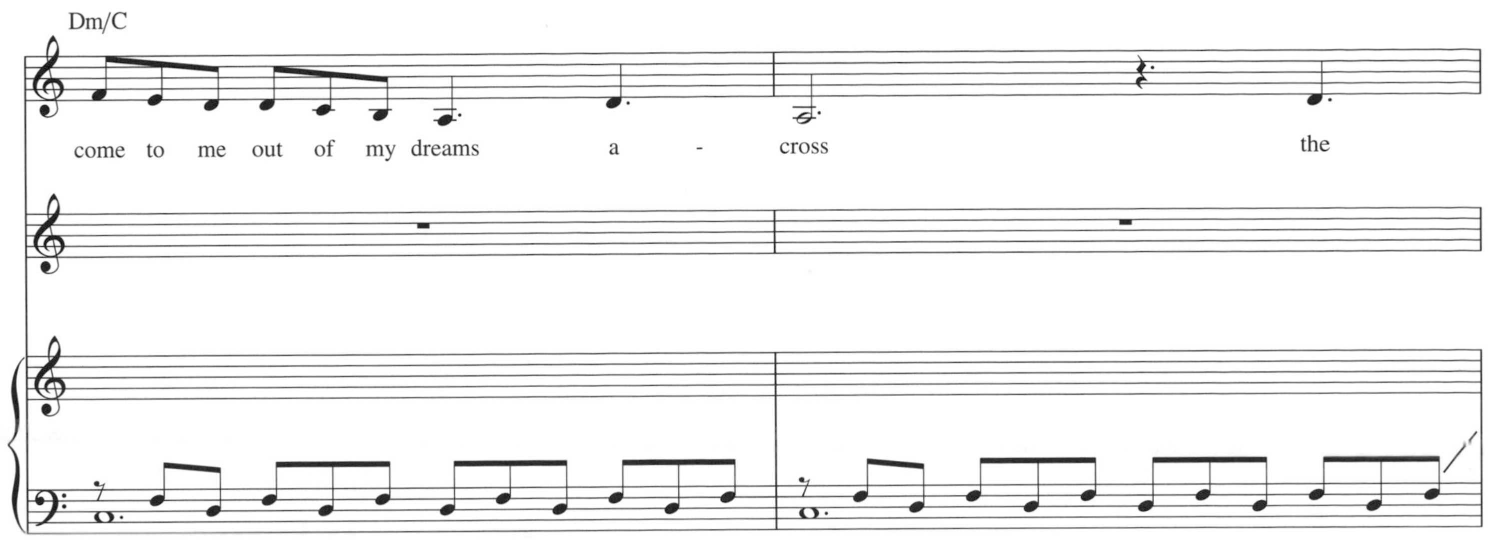
Dm/C
come to me out of my dreams a - cross the

C
night.
C
You take my
8va
mp
R.H.
L.H.

Dm/C
C/B
hand, though you may be so man - y stars a -

Am
Dm/C
way.
I
know that our spir - its and souls are
loco

A♭/C
We've
cir - cled the moon and we've touched the
one.

C
D
G
sun.
So
here
we'll
stay.
For
So
here
we'll
stay.
For

G
G/F♯
Em7
al - ways, for - ev - er, be -
al - ways, for - ev - er, be -
mf
Am/G
yond here and on to e - ter - ni - ty. For
yond here and on to e - ter - ni - ty. For
G
G/F♯
Em7
al - ways, for - ev - er, for
al - ways, for - ev - er, for

Am/G
B♭6/F
us there's no time and no space.
Wher -
us there's no time and no space,
no bar - ri - er love won't e - rase.
R.H.
A♭/E♭
Cm/G
D
ev - er you go I still know in my heart you will be with
with
R.H.
G
C
me.
me.
From this day
8va
loco

Gsus4/C
C
G/B
Day
on,
on
I'm
cer - tain that I'll nev - er
be
a -
(8va)
loco
8va
Am
Dm/C
da
da,
I
know what my heart must have al - ways
lone,
(8va)
known,
that
Ab/C
love has a pow - er that's all
its
know what my heart must have known,
love has a pow - er that's all
its
(8va)

A♭/G
E♭/F
Fm
Cadd9
C
Am7
own. And for al - ways, for - ev - er,
own. And for al - ways, for - ev - er,
(8va)
loco
f

Dm/C
Cadd9
C
C/B
now we can fly. And for al - ways and
now we can fly. And for al - ways and

Am7
Am/G
F
F/E
al - ways we will go on be -
al - ways we will go on
R.H.

Dm7
C
yond good - bye.
For
good - bye.
dim.
mp
C
Am7
al - ways,
be -
for - ev - er,
p
R.H.
L.H.
Dm/C
yond here and on to e - ter - ni - ty.
For

C
C/B
Am7
Am/G
4
and ev - er you'll be a
al - ways
8va
loco
F
F/E
Dm7
C/G
part of me. And for al - ways, for-
you'll be a part of me. And for al - ways, for-
cresc.
mf
f
2
2
Am7
Dm/C
ev - er, a thou-sand to-mor-rows may cross the
ev - er, a thou-sand to-mor-rows may cross the
8va

C
C/B
sky and for al - ways and
sky and for al - ways and
loco
Am7
Am/G
F
F/E
al - ways we will go on be -
al - ways we will go on
Dm
Dm7
C
yond good - bye.
good - bye.
dim.
mp
R.H.
rit.
L.H.
R.H.

For You

Words and Music by
John Denver

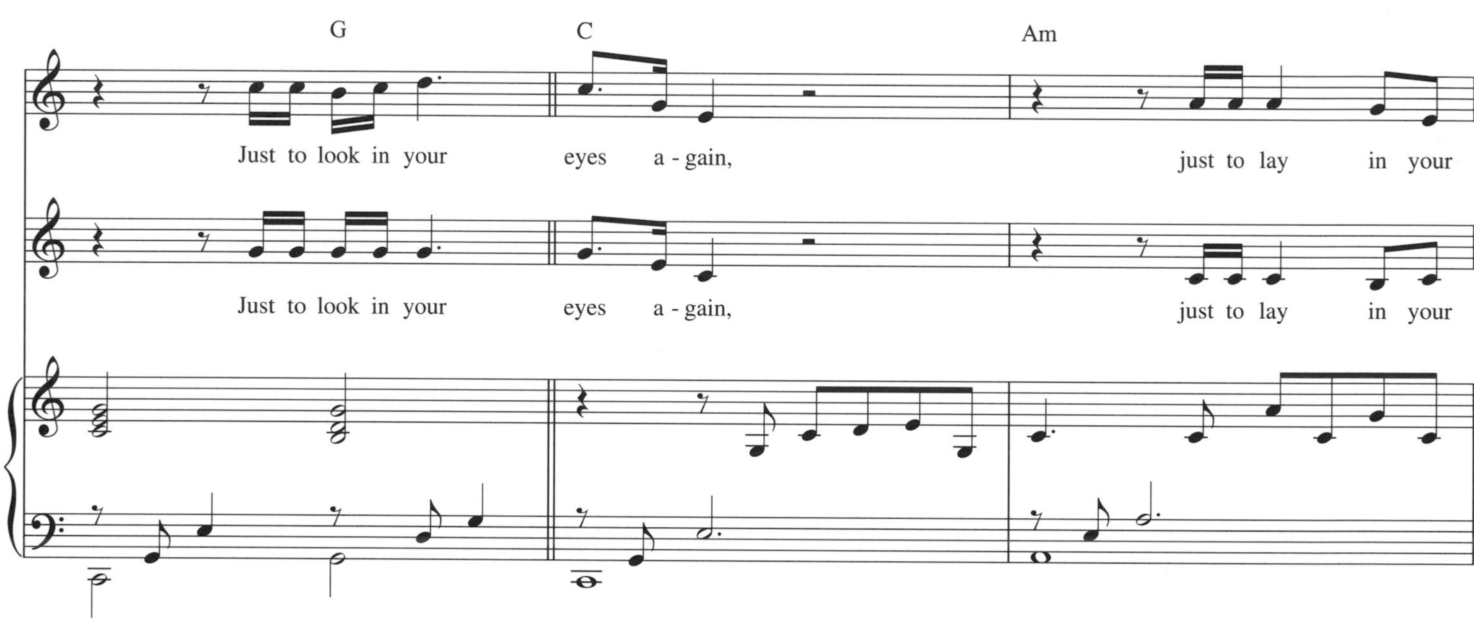

C
G
C
you.
Just to live in your laugh - ter,
you.
Just to live in your laugh - ter,

Am
F
Dm
just to sing in your heart,
just to be ev - 'ry one
just to sing in your heart,
just to be ev - 'ry one

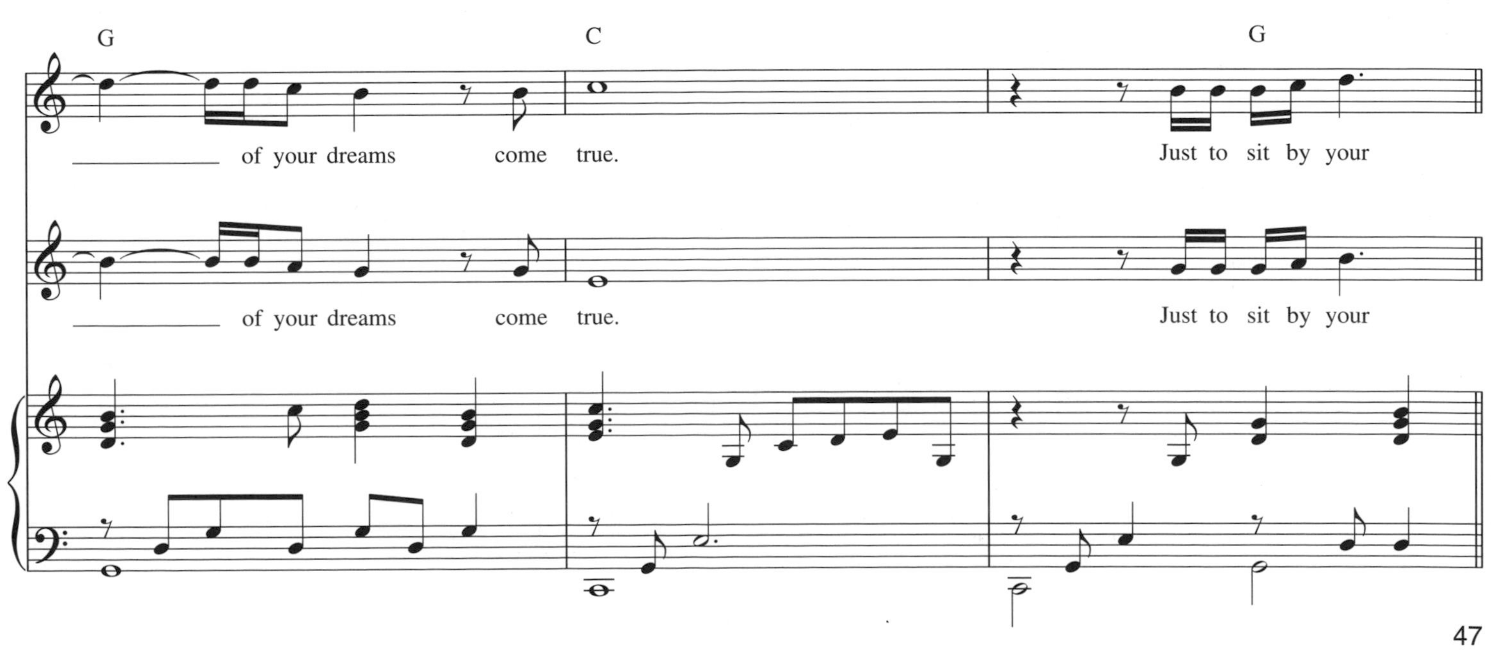
G
C
G
of your dreams come true.
Just to sit by your
of your dreams come true.
Just to sit by your

C
Am
F
win - dow, just to touch in the night,
morn - ing, just you by my side,
win - dow, just to touch in the night,
morn - ing, just you by my side,
(mp)
Dm
G
C
just to of - fer a pray'r each day for you.
just to know that you're nev - er real - ly far a - way.
just to of - fer a pray'r each day for you.
just to know that you're nev - er real - ly far a - way.
G
C
Am
Just to long for your kiss - es, just to dream of your
Just a rea - son for liv - ing, just to say I a -
Just to long for your kiss - es, just to dream of your
Just a rea - son for liv - ing, just to say I a -

F
Dm
G
sighs,
dore,
just to know
just to know
that I'd
that you're
give
here
my
in my
life
heart
for
to
C
G
C
you.
stay.
For
you,
all the
cresc.
mf
Am
F
G
C
Am
F
G
rest of my life;
for
you,
all the
best of my life;
for

1.
C
G
C
you a - lone,
on - ly for you.
you a - lone,
on - ly for you.

2.
G
C
G
C
Just to wake up each
you.
Just to wake up each
you.
dim.

Am
F
Dm
G

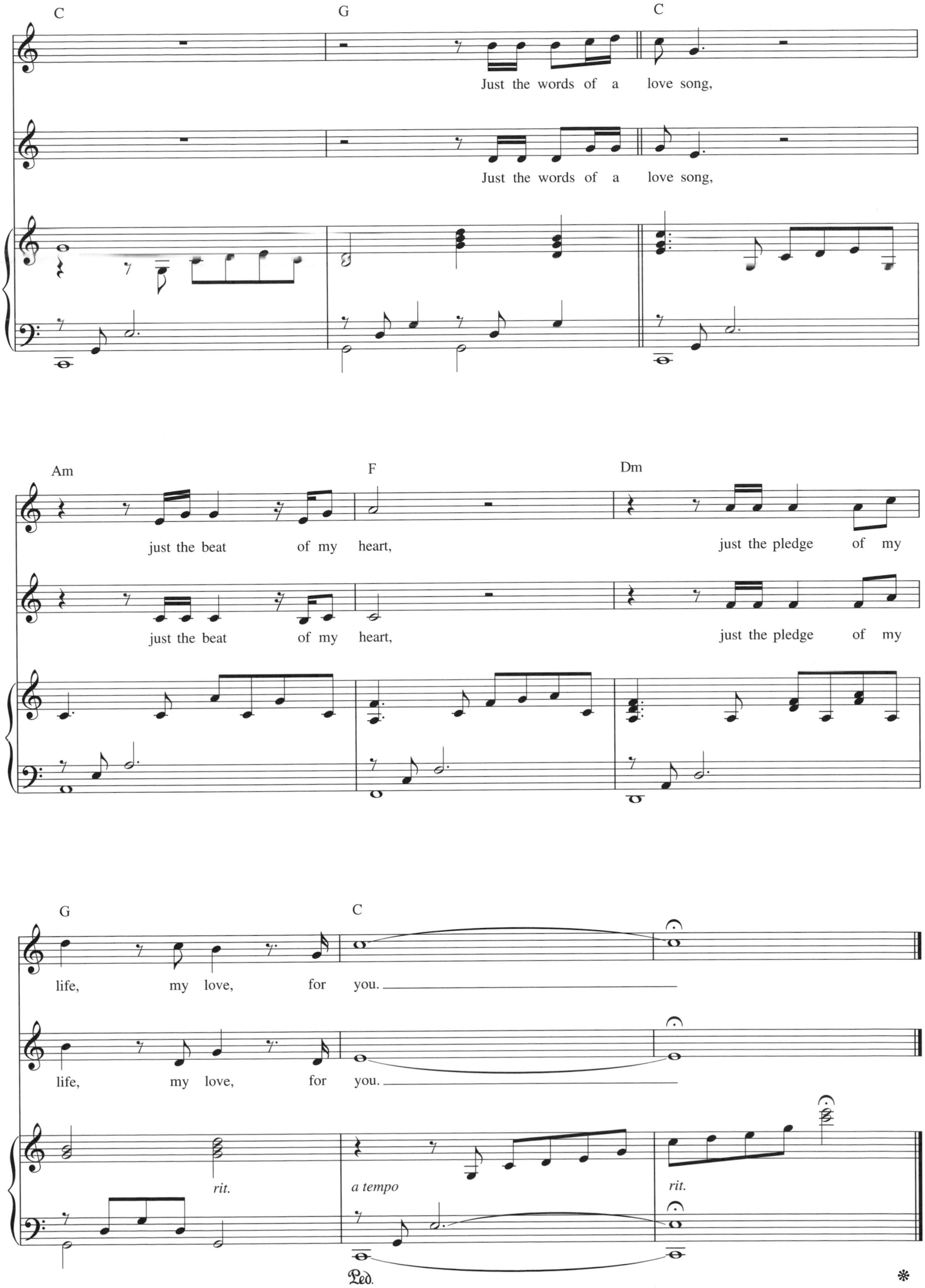

C G C
Just the words of a love song,
Just the words of a love song,
Am F Dm
just the beat of my heart, just the pledge of my
just the beat of my heart, just the pledge of my
G C
life, my love, for you.
life, my love, for you.
rit.
a tempo
rit.
Ped.

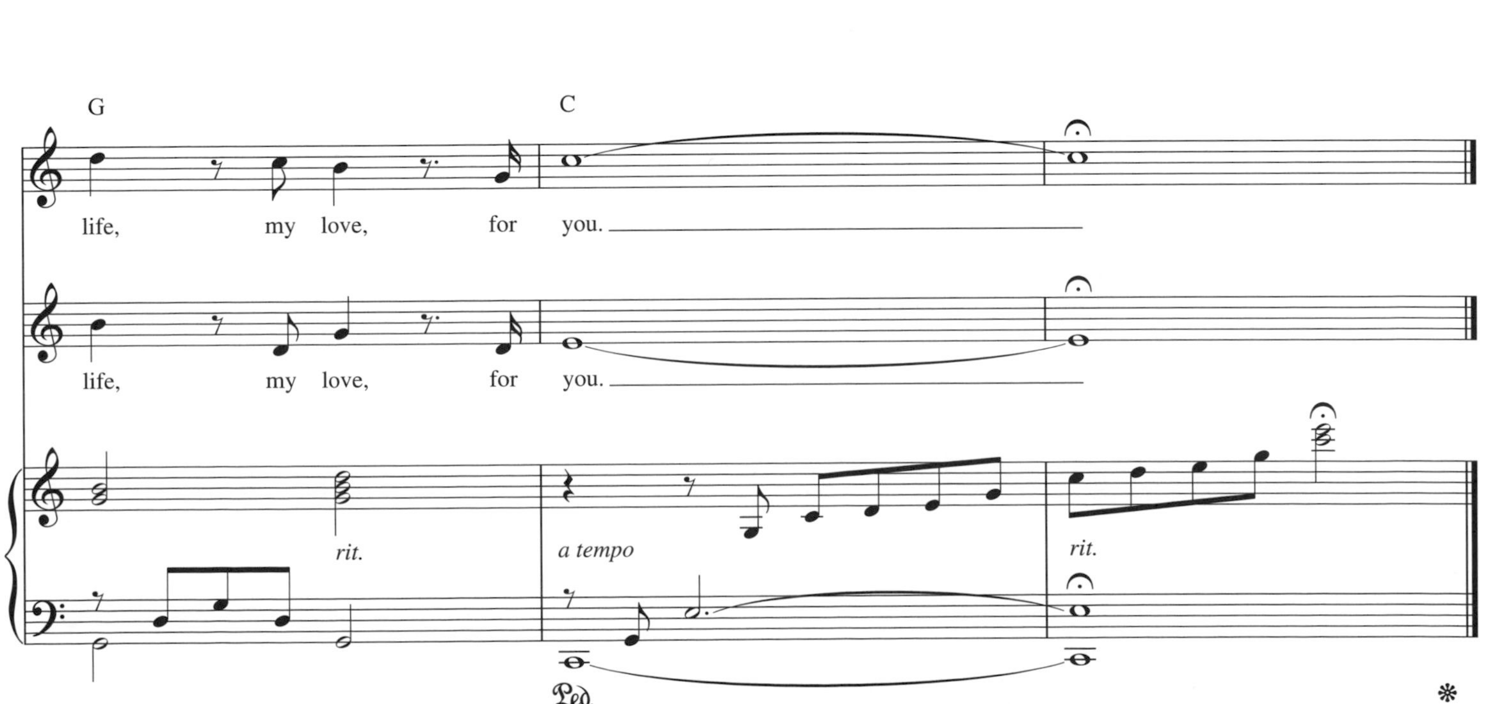

Give Me Forever
(I Do)

Words and Music by
Carter Cathcart, John Tesh,
Juni Morrison and James Ingram

Moderately fast
mf
with pedal
C
Fmaj7
B♭
Dm7
C/G
F♯m7♭5
Fmaj7
Dm7/G
Cadd2
C
G/B
Look - ing out, I see,
With this ring I'm bound,
(melody)
Look - ing out, I see,
With this ring I'm bound,

Am
Fadd2
and I know just how much you're a
and I prom - ise that I'll nev - er
and I know just how much you're a
and I prom - ise that I'll nev - er
Dm7add4
Gsus4
G
Cadd2
part of me. I see you and I
let you down. To fam - 'ly and friends
part of me. I see you and I
let you down. To fam - 'ly and friends
Gadd2/B
Gadd2
G
to - geth - er in life, so there's
and the Lord up a - bove, I will
to - geth - er in life, so there's
and the Lord up a - bove, I will

C Bb/D C/E F F#m7b5
noth - ing I would - n't do to make you my
swear I'll be true to you and give you my
noth - ing I would - n't do to make you my
swear I'll be true to you and give you my

Gsus4 G Esus4 E/G#
wife.
love.
Won't you give me for - ev - er to
wife.
love.
Won't you give me for - ev - er to

Am D7sus4 D/F#
show all of the love I
show all of the love I have here for

G7sus4
G
Am7
G/B
C
Esus4
E
have here for you.
Give me my rea - son for
you.
And if you give me my rea - son for
To Coda
Am
D7/F♯
F
G
liv - ing, to love you, I love you, I
liv - ing, to love you, I love you, I
1.
C
Fmaj7
B♭maj7
Dm7
do.
do.
3
3
3

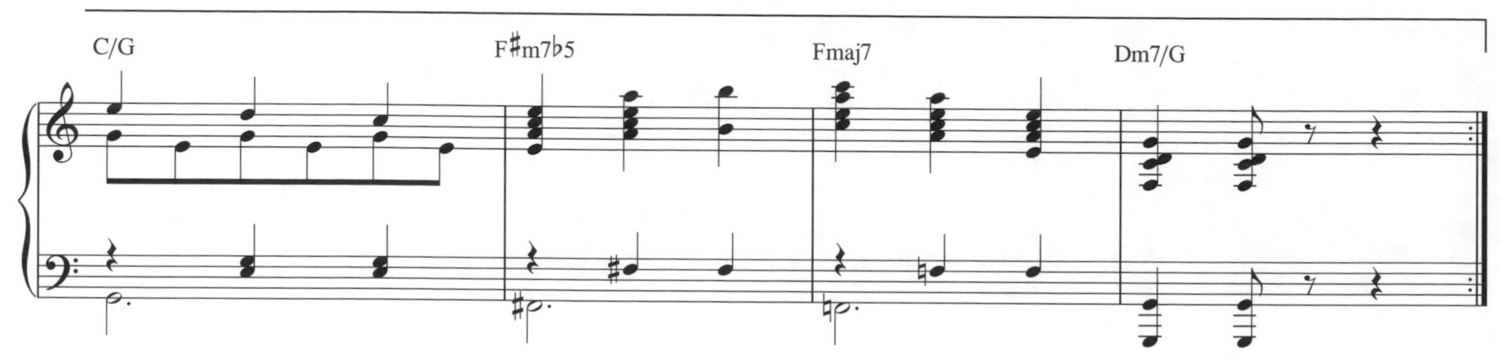
C/G
F♯m7♭5
Fmaj7
Dm7/G

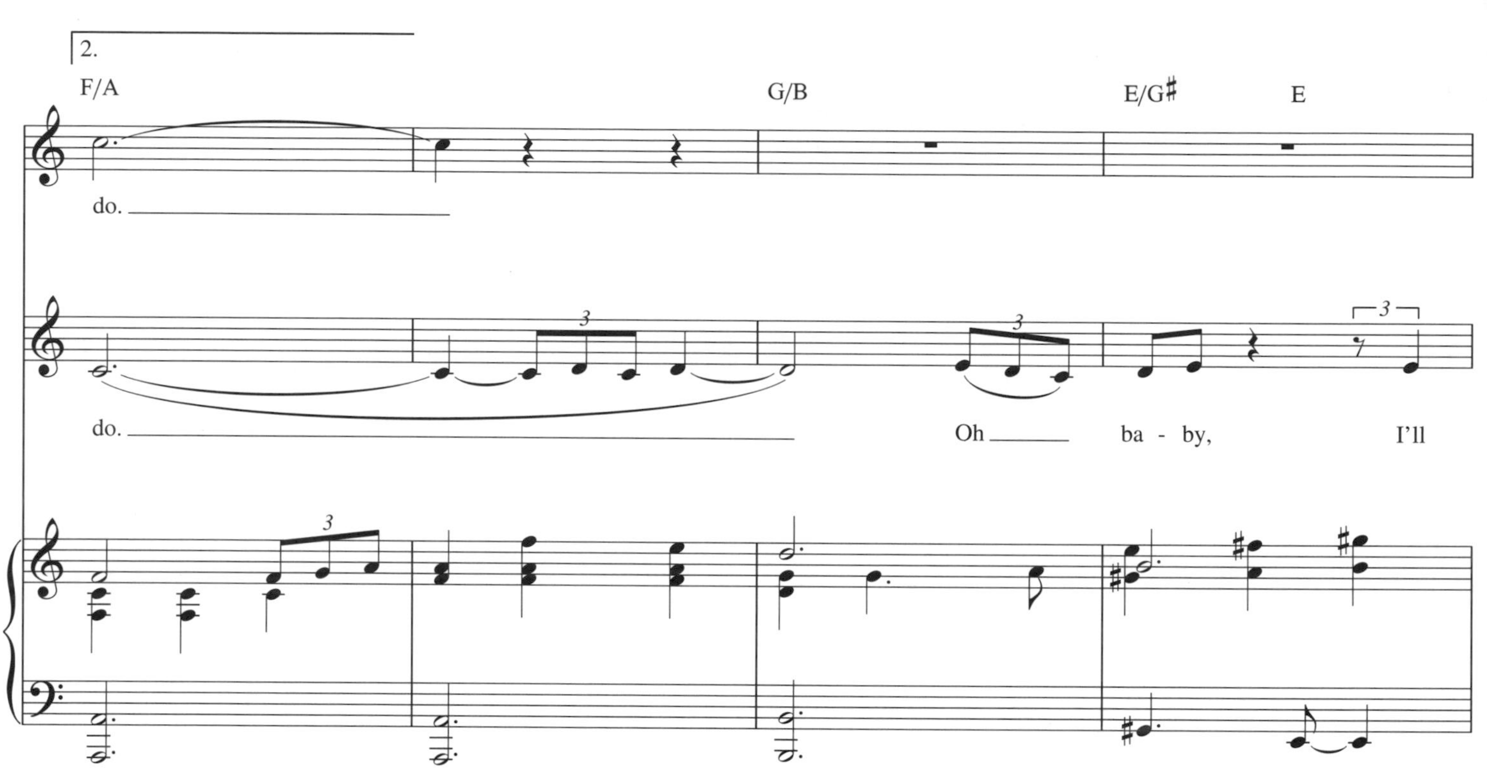
2.
F/A
G/B
E/G♯
E
do.
do.
Oh baby, I'll

Am
G/B
F/C
C
Dm
C/E
G/B
I love you forever and ever, oh, I
love you forever and ever, oh, I
8va
loco

F/A
G/B
E/G♯
do.
do.
D.S. al Coda
Am
D/F♯
Gsus4
G
Won't you
Won't you
Coda
Am
D/F♯
F
G
do. To love you.
do. To love you, I love you, I

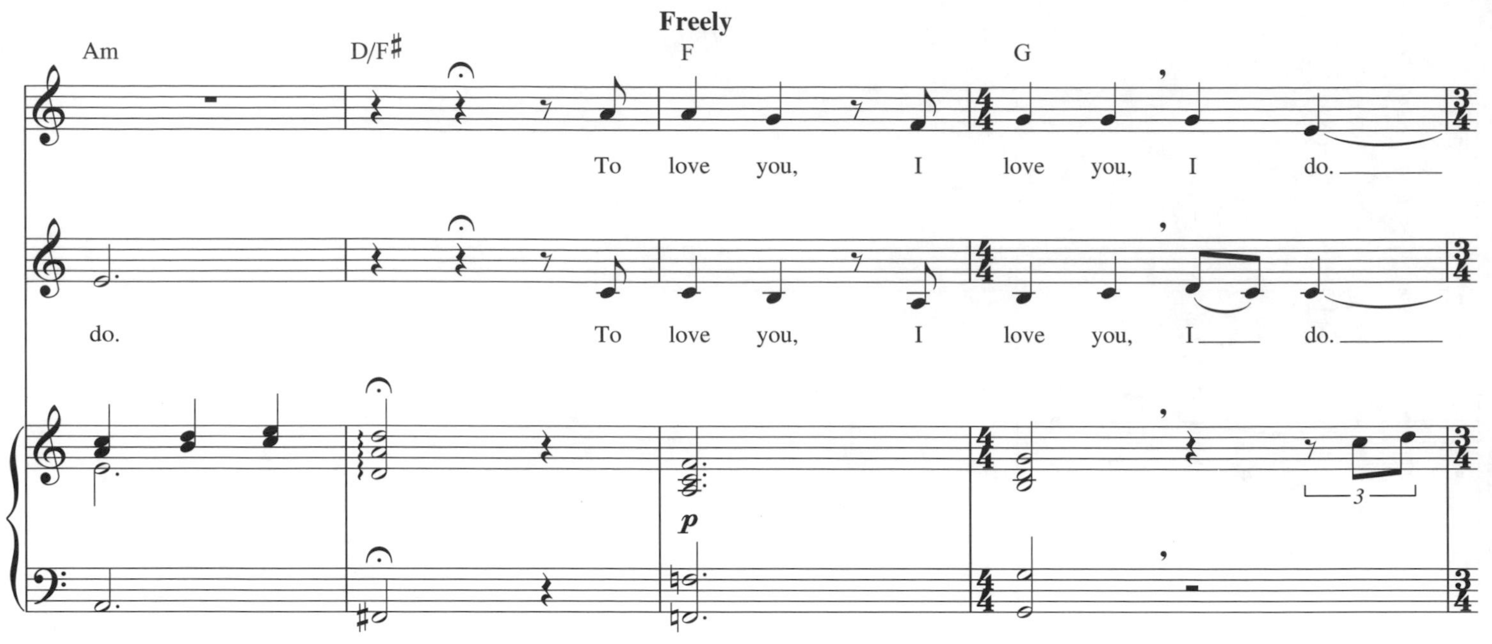
Freely
Am
D/F♯
F
G
To love you, I love you, I do.
do.
To love you, I love you, I do.
p

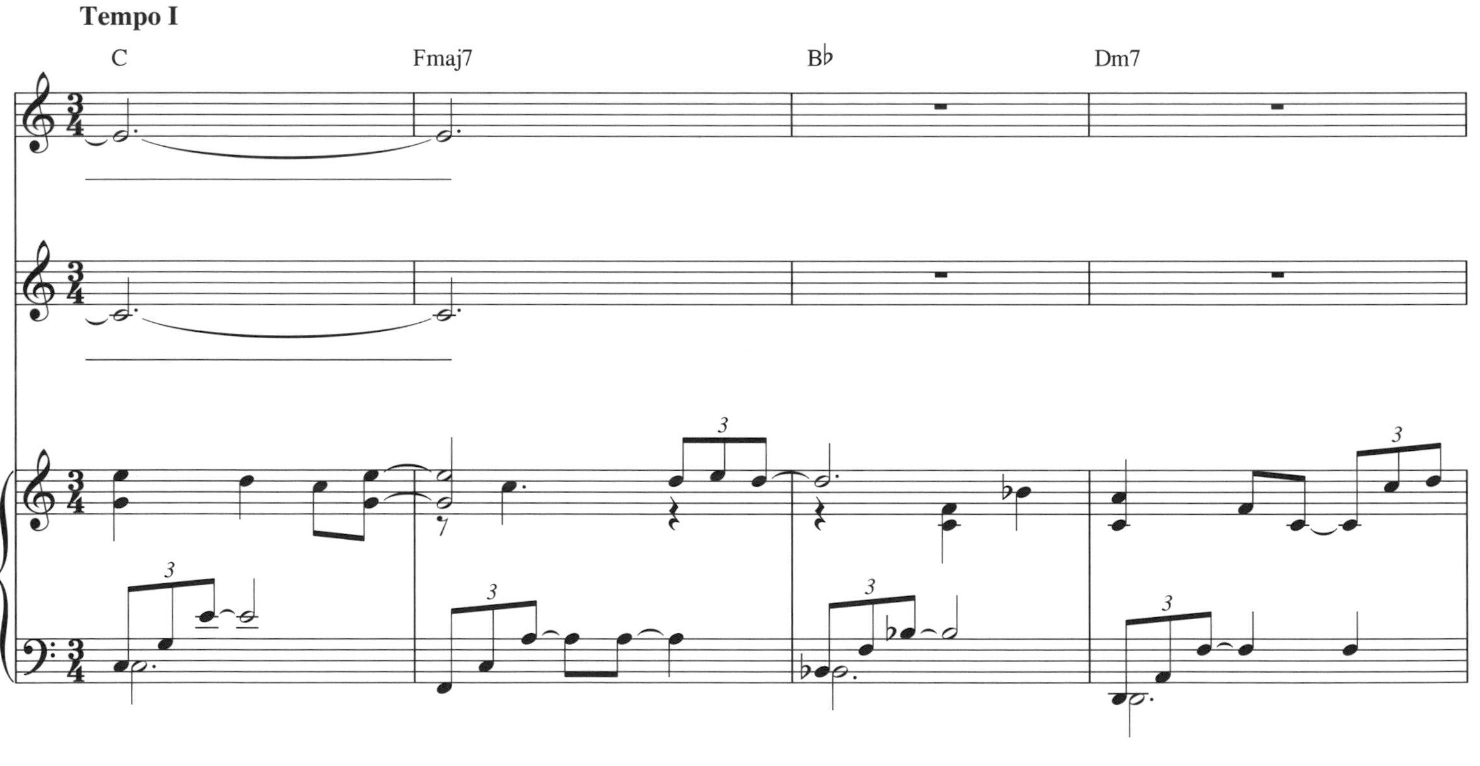
Tempo I
C
Fmaj7
B♭
Dm7

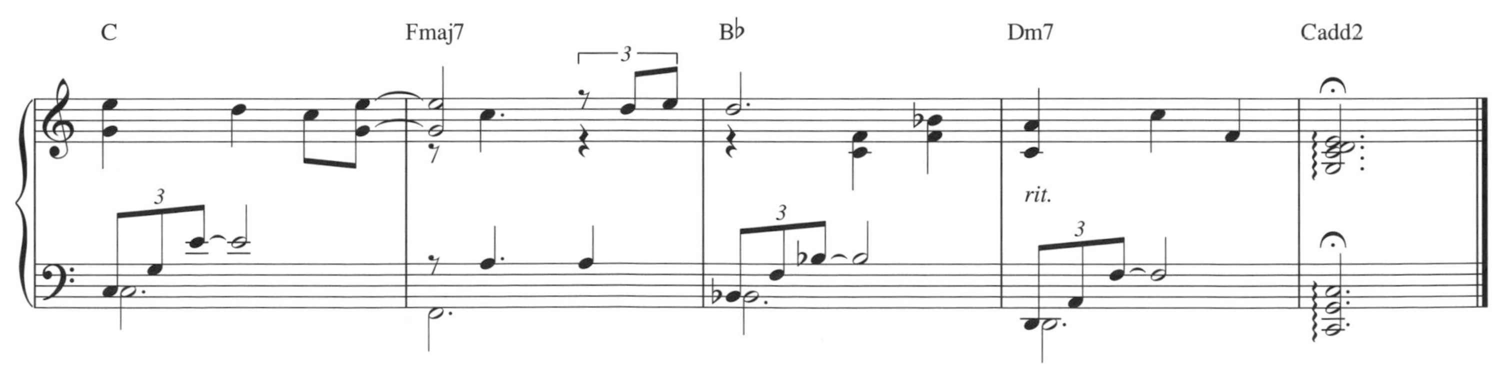
C
Fmaj7
B♭
Dm7
Cadd2
rit.

I Love You Truly

Words and Music by
Carrie Jacobs-Bond

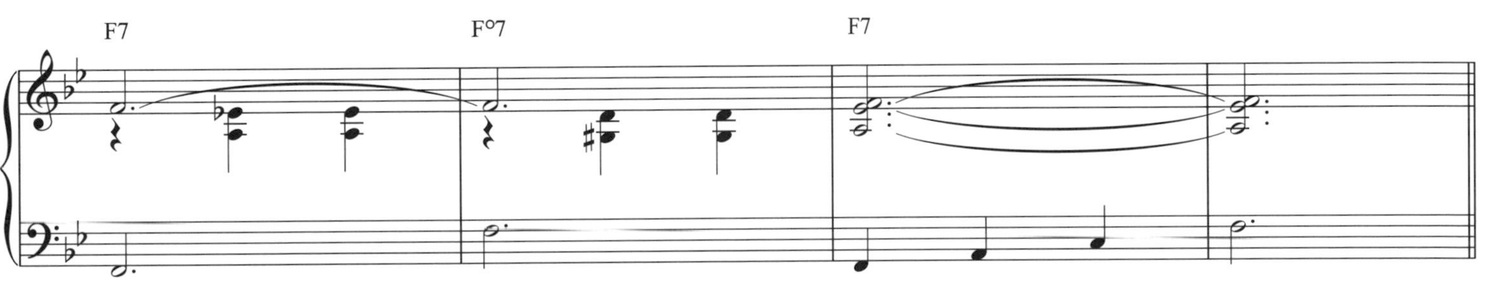

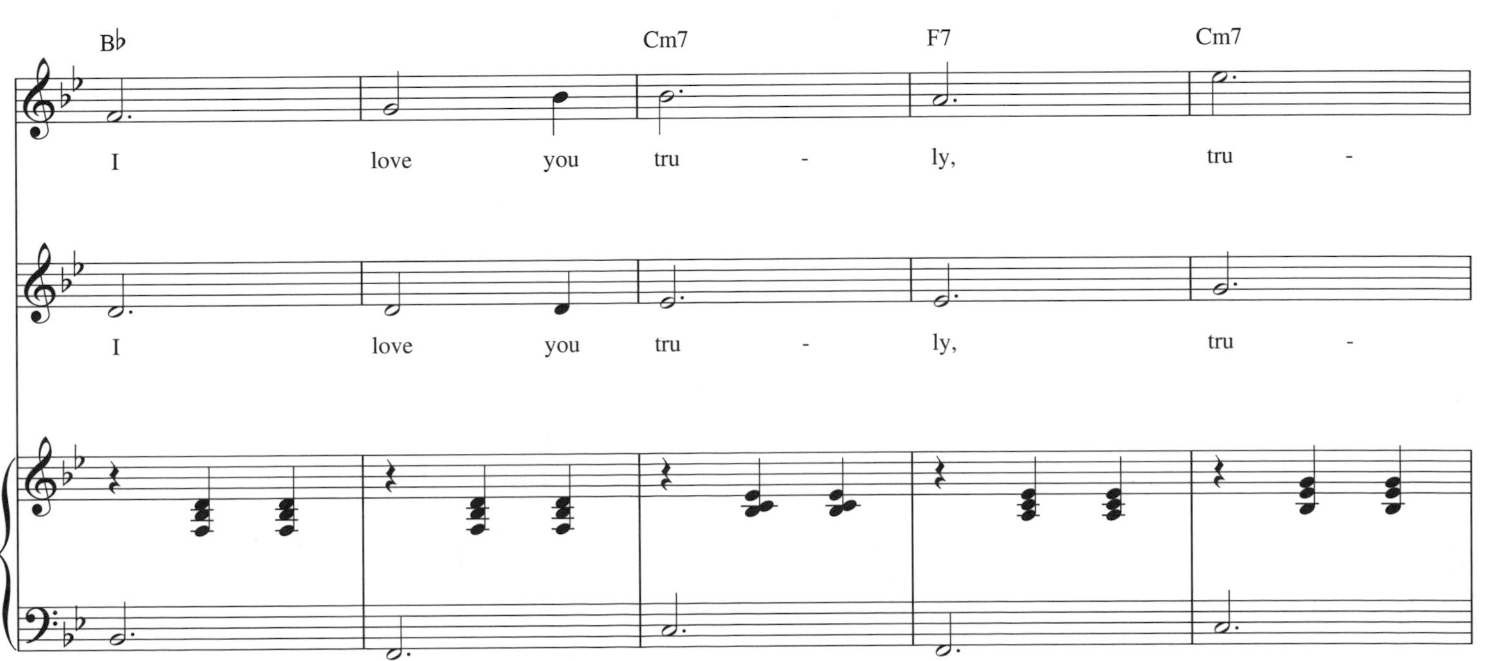

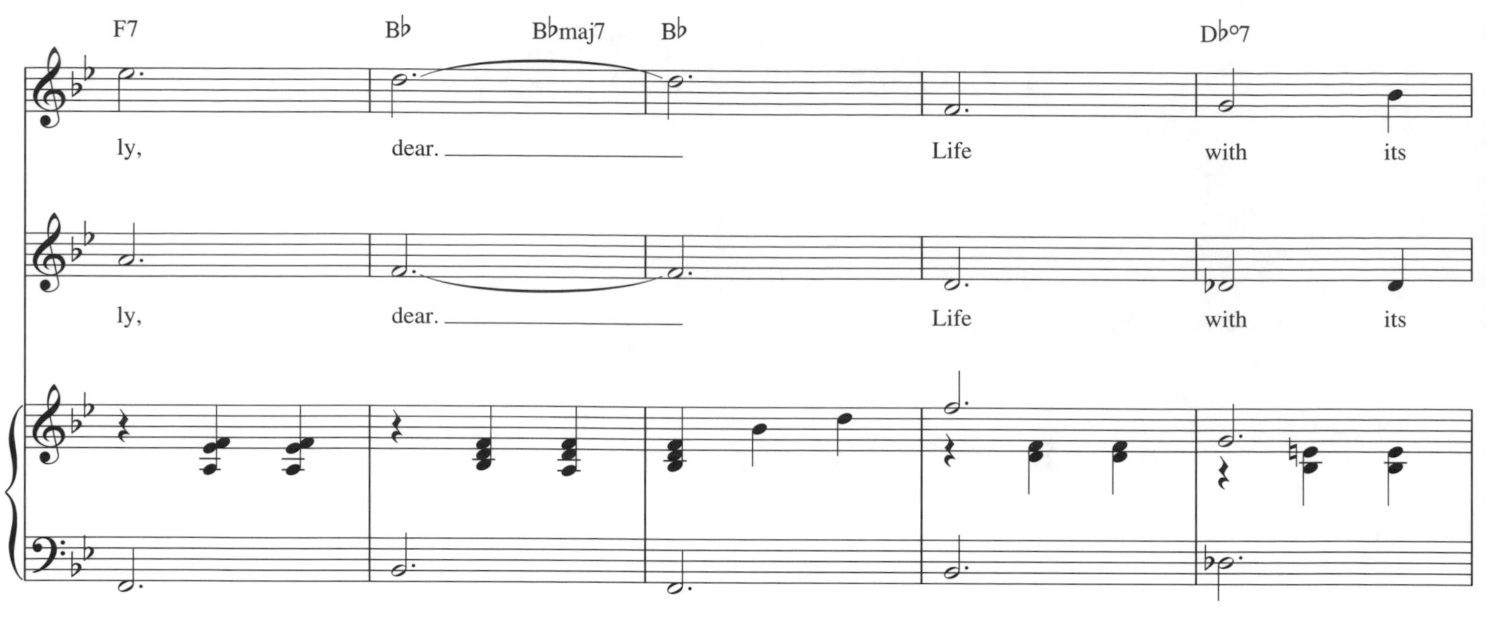
F7
B♭
B♭maj7
B♭
D♭°7
ly, dear. Life with its
ly, dear. Life with its

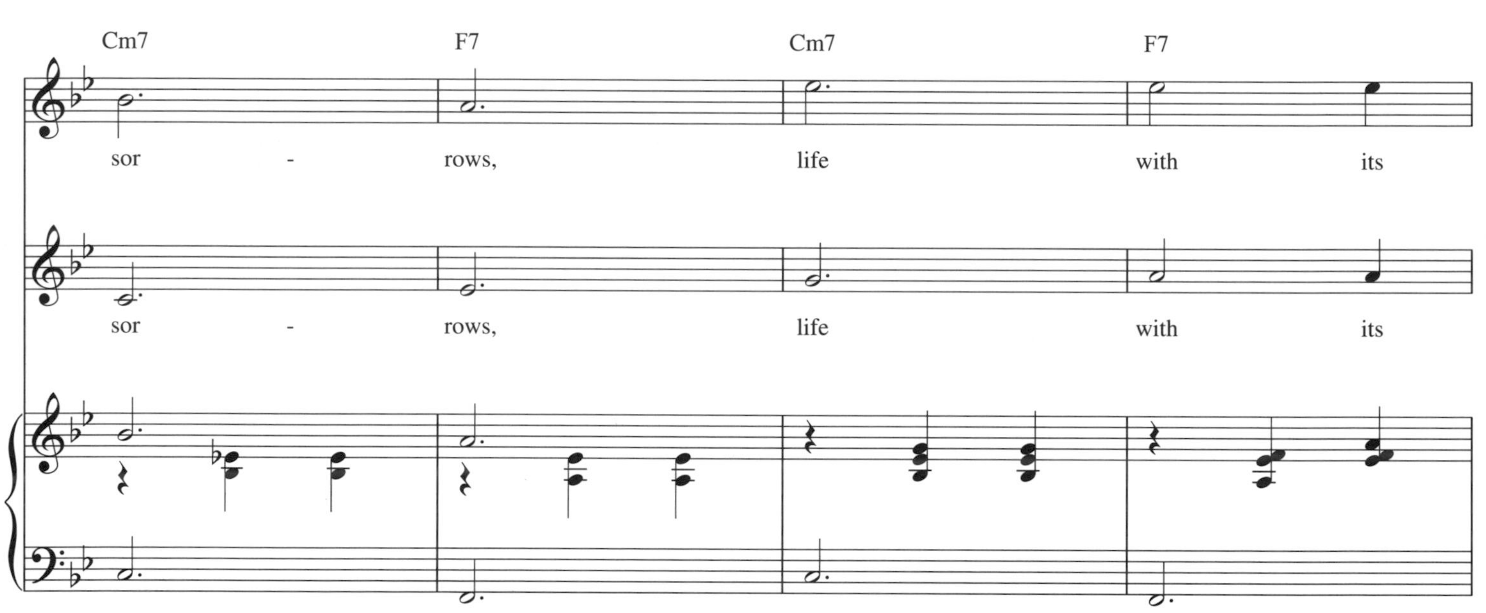
Cm7
F7
Cm7
F7
sor - rows, life with its
sor - rows, life with its

B♭
B♭maj7
B♭
D7
Gm
tears, fades in - to dreams
tears, fades in - to dreams

Gm/F
E°7
when I feel you are near.
when I feel you are near.
B♭
D7
For I love you tru -
For I love you tru -
G7
Cm7
F7
B♭
ly, tru - ly, dear.
ly, tru - ly, dear.

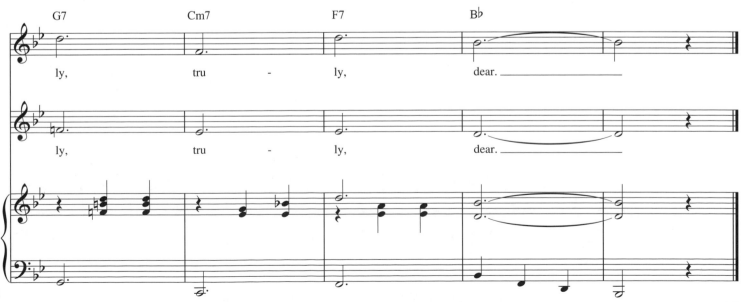

Laudate Dominum
from VESPERAE SOLENNES

By Wolfgang Amadeus Mozart

tr
te Do - mi - num o - mnes
te Do - mi - num o - mnes
tr
tr
gen - tes, lau - da - te
gen - tes, lau - da - te
tr
e - um o -
e - um o -

mnes po - pu - li.
mnes po - pu - li.
Quo - ni-am con - fir - ma - ta est su - per
Quo - ni-am con - fir - ma - ta est su - per
nos mi - se - ri - cor - di-a
nos mi - se - ri - cor - di-a

e - jus, et
e - jus, et
ve - ri-tas ve - ri-tas Do - mi-ni
ve - ri-tas ve - ri-tas Do - mi - ni
ma - net, ma - net
ma - net, ma - net

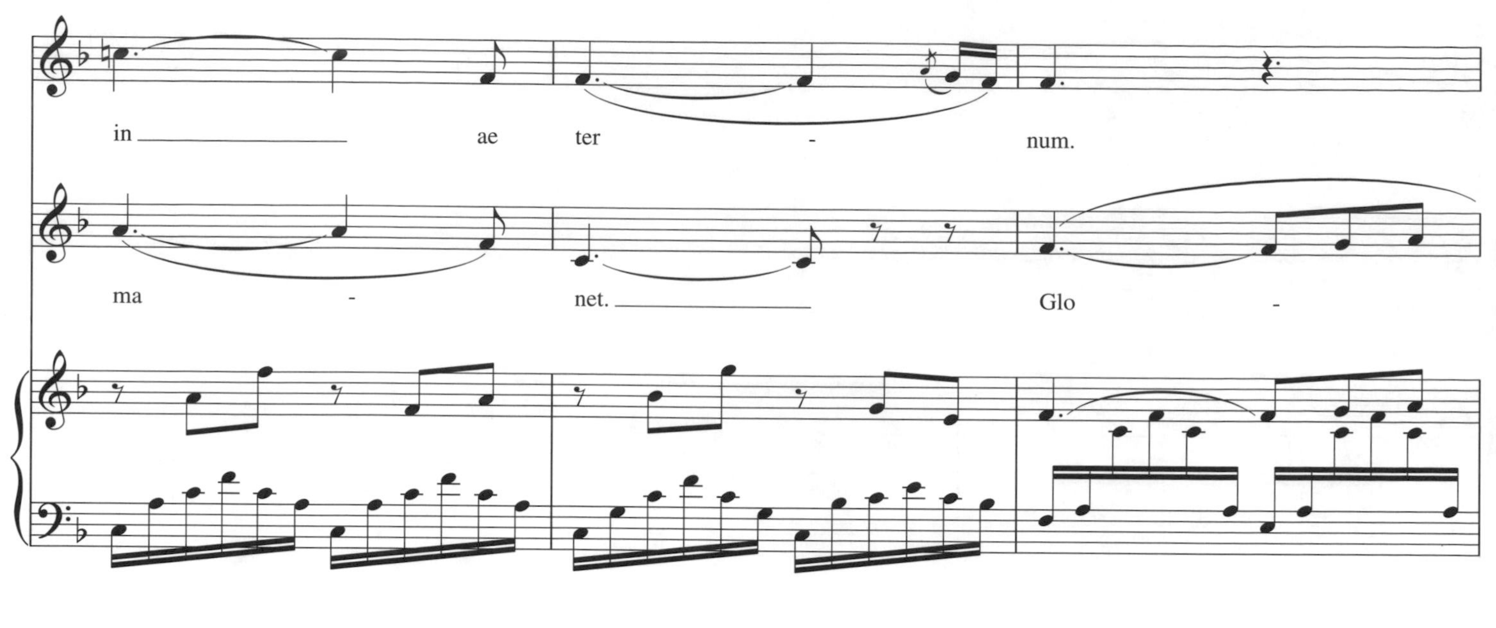
in ae ter - num.
ma - net. Glo -

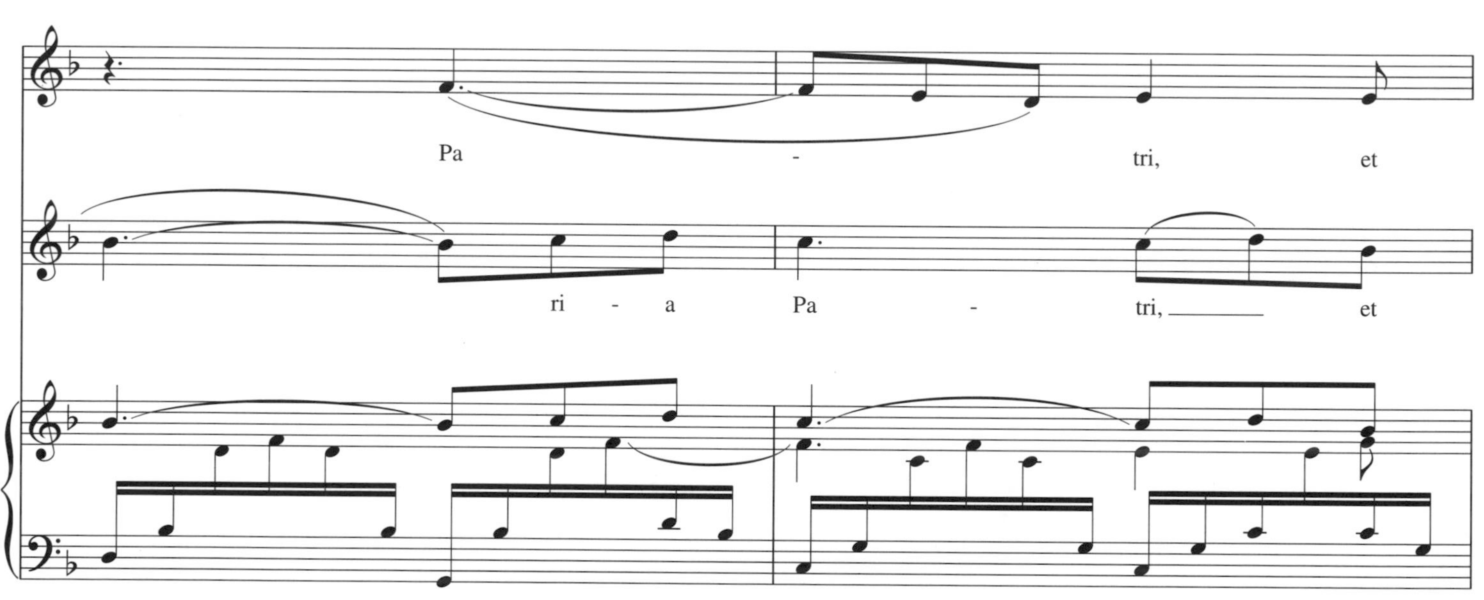
Pa - tri, et
ri - a Pa - tri, et

tr
Fi - li - o, et Spi - ri - tu - i San - cto,
tr
Fi - li - o, et Spi - ri - tu - i San - cto,
tr
tr

Si - cut
Si - cut
e - rat in prin -
e - rat in prin -
ci - pi - o, et nunc, — et
ci - pi - o, et nunc, et

sem - per, et in sae - cu - la
sem - per, et in sae - cu - la
sae - cu - lo -
sae - cu - lo -
rum. A-, A -
rum. A - men.

men,
a
-
A
-
men.
tr
men.
A
-
men.
A
-
men.
A
-
men.

Longer

Words and Music by
Dan Fogelberg

Moderately, gently

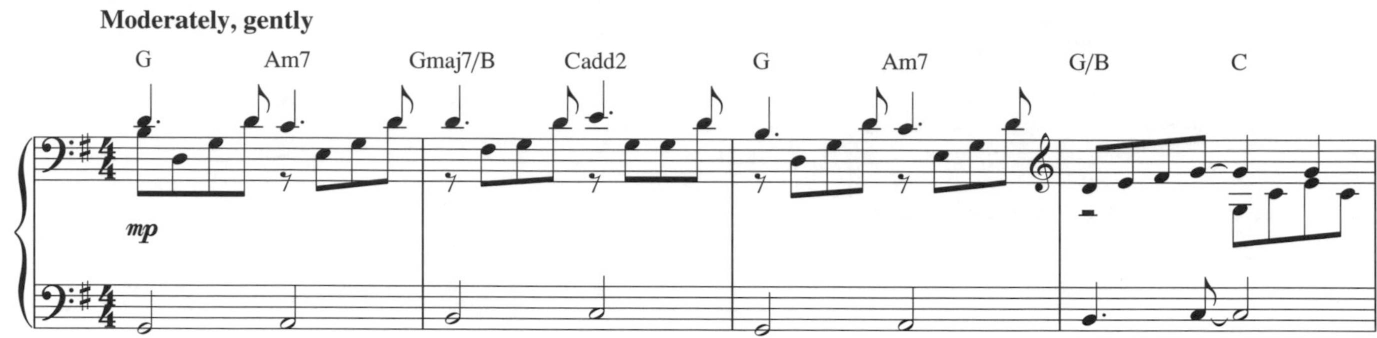
G
Am7
Gmaj7/B
Cadd2
G
Am7
G/B
C
mp

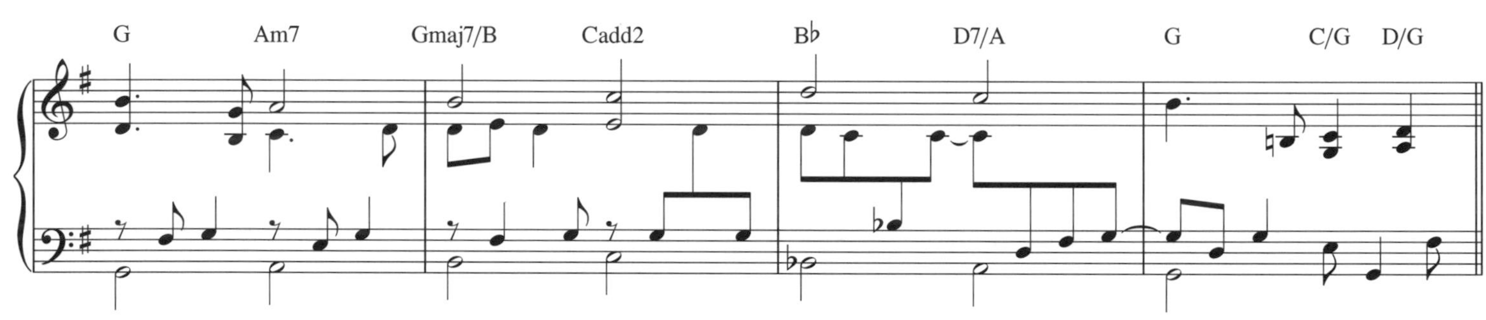
G
Am7
Gmaj7/B
Cadd2
B♭
D7/A
G
C/G
D/G

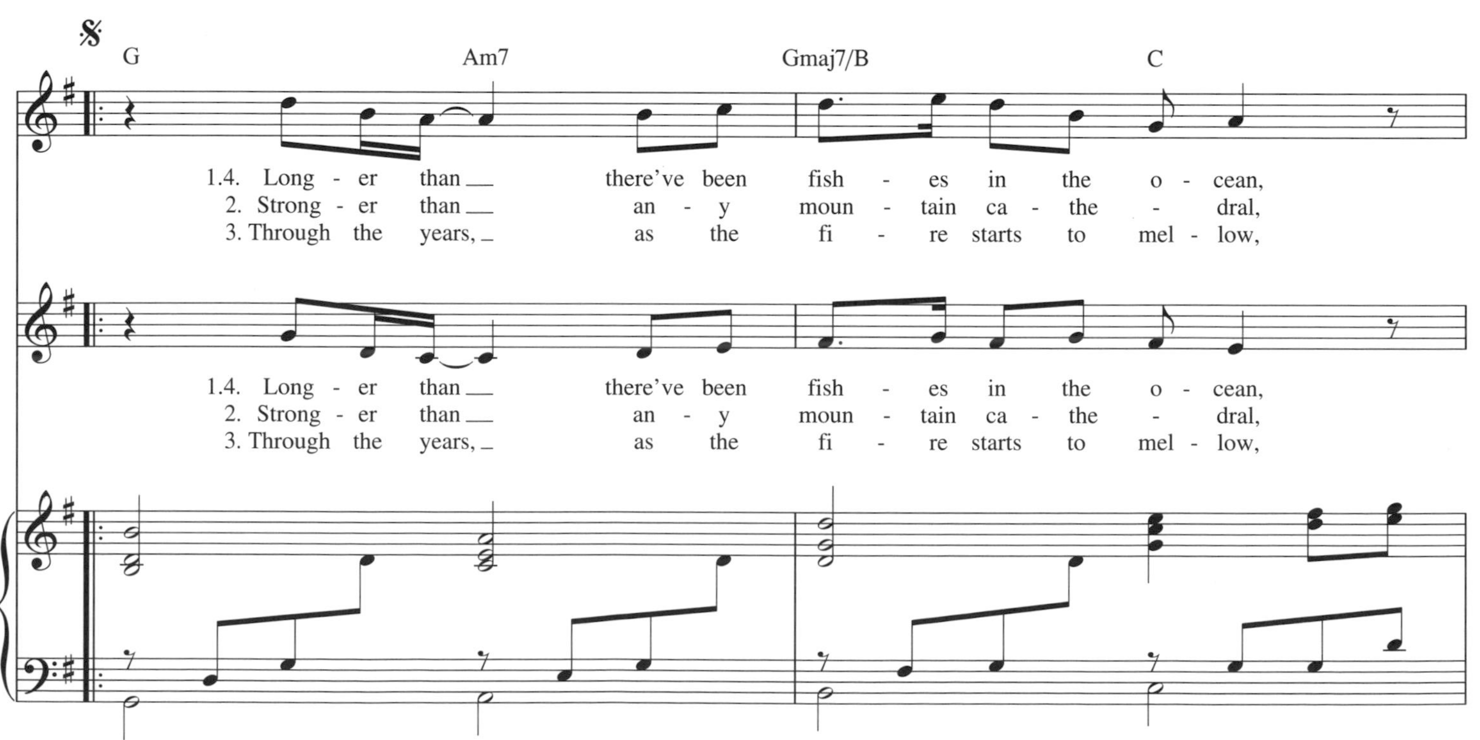
G
Am7
Gmaj7/B
C
1.4. Long - er than there've been fish - es in the o - cean,
2. Strong - er than an - y moun - tain ca - the - dral,
3. Through the years, as the fi - re starts to mel - low,
1.4. Long - er than there've been fish - es in the o - cean,
2. Strong - er than an - y moun - tain ca - the - dral,
3. Through the years, as the fi - re starts to mel - low,

G
Am7
Gmaj7/B
C
high - er than any - y bird ev - er flew,
tru - er than an - y tree ev - er grew,
burn - ing lines in the book of our lives, though the
high - er than any - y bird ev - er flew,
tru - er than an - y tree ev - er grew,
burn - ing lines in the book of our lives, though the
G
Am7
Gmaj7/B
C
long - er than there've been stars up in the heav - ens,
deep - er than an - y for - est pri - me - val,
bind - ing cracks and the pag - es start to yel - low,
long - er than there've been stars up in the heav - ens,
deep - er than an - y for - est pri - me - val,
bind - ing cracks and the pag - es start to yel - low,
To Codas I & II
1.
B♭
D7/A
G
C/G
D/G
I've been in love with you.
I am in love with you.
I'll be in love with you.
I've been in love with you.
I am in love with you.
I'll be in love with you.

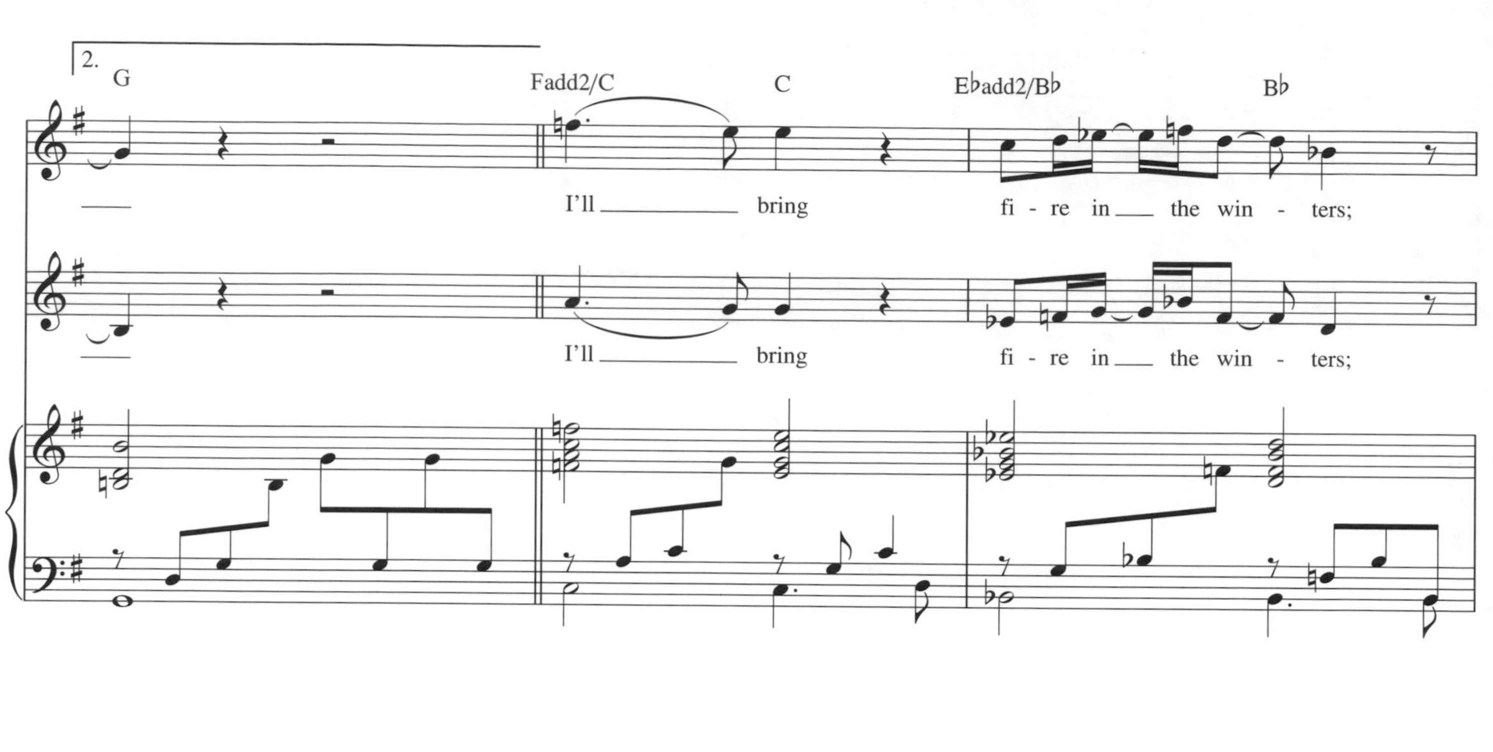
2.
G
Fadd2/C
C
E♭add2/B♭
B♭
I'll bring fi - re in the win - ters;
I'll bring fi - re in the win - ters;

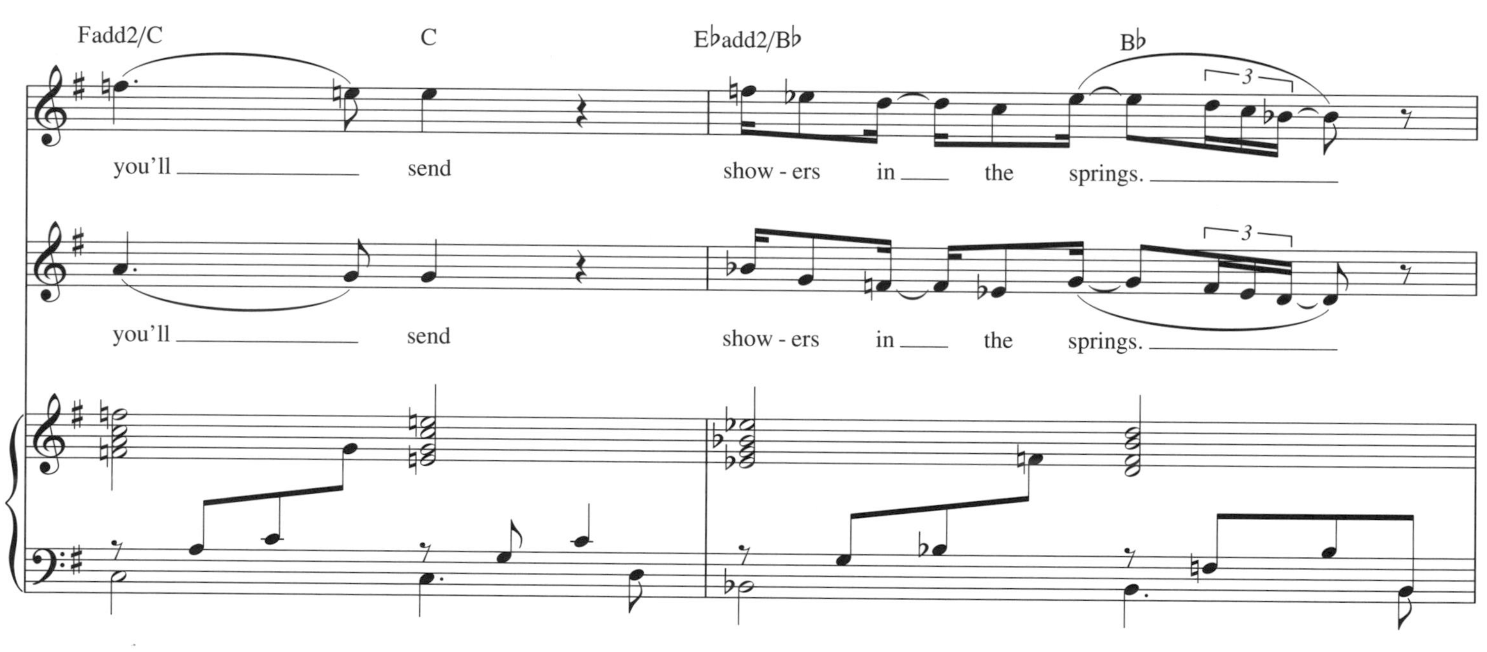
Fadd2/C
C
E♭add2/B♭
B♭
you'll send show - ers in the springs.
you'll send show - ers in the springs.

Fadd2/C
C
E♭add2/B♭
B♭
We'll fly through the falls and sum - mers with
We'll fly through the falls and sum - mers with

D.S. al Coda I

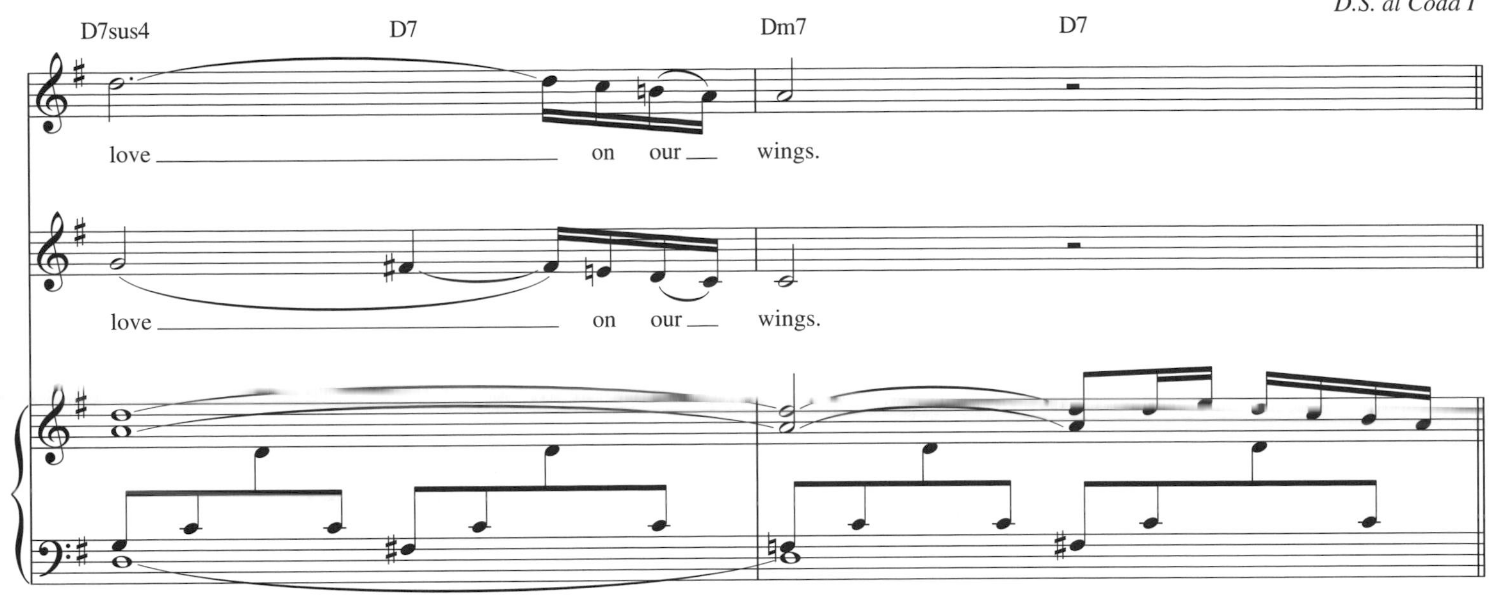
D7sus4
D7
Dm7
D7
love on our wings.
love on our wings.

Coda I
G
B♭
D7/A
I'll be in love with you.
I'll be in love with you.

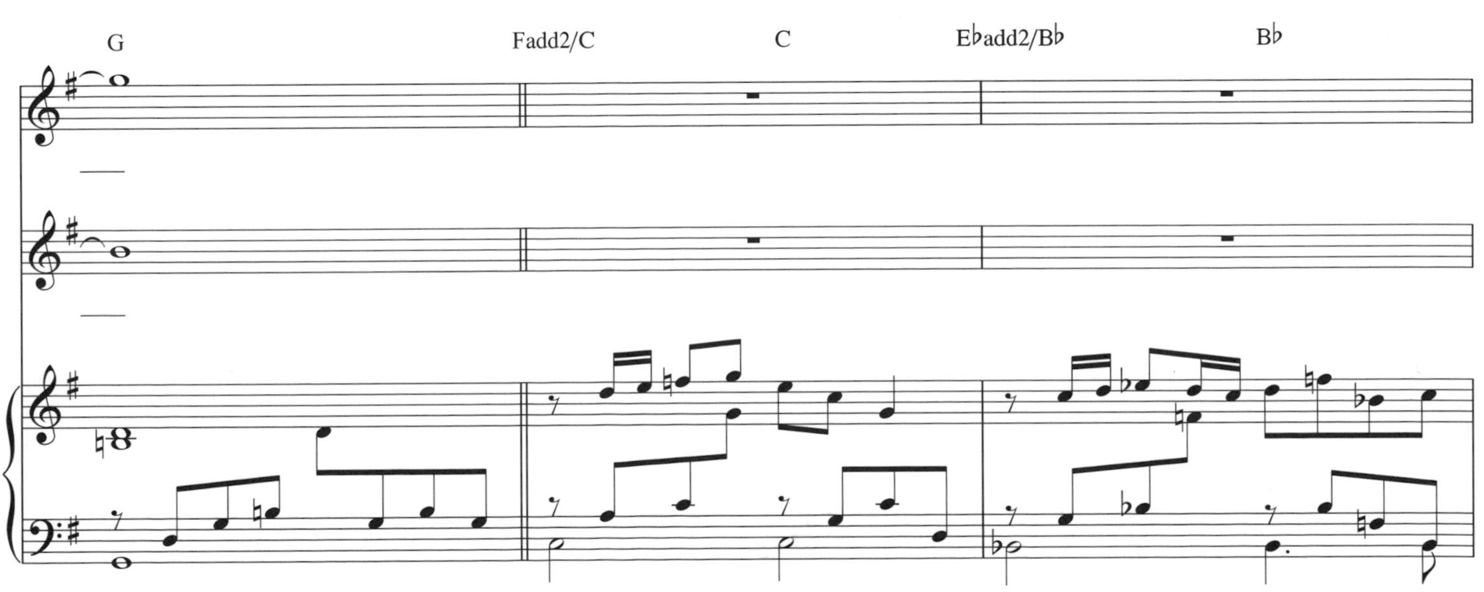
G
Fadd2/C
C
E♭add2/B♭
B♭

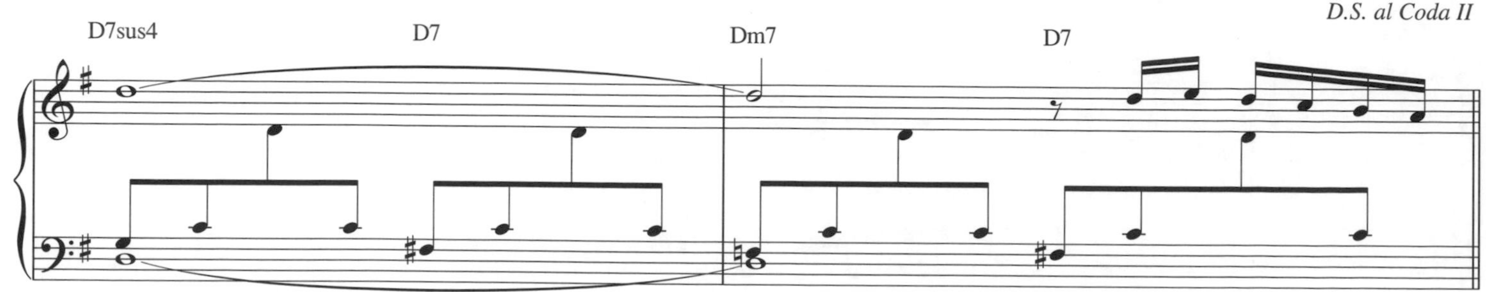
D.S. al Coda II
D7sus4
D7
Dm7
D7

Coda II
G
B♭
D7/A
I am in love with you.
I am in love with you.

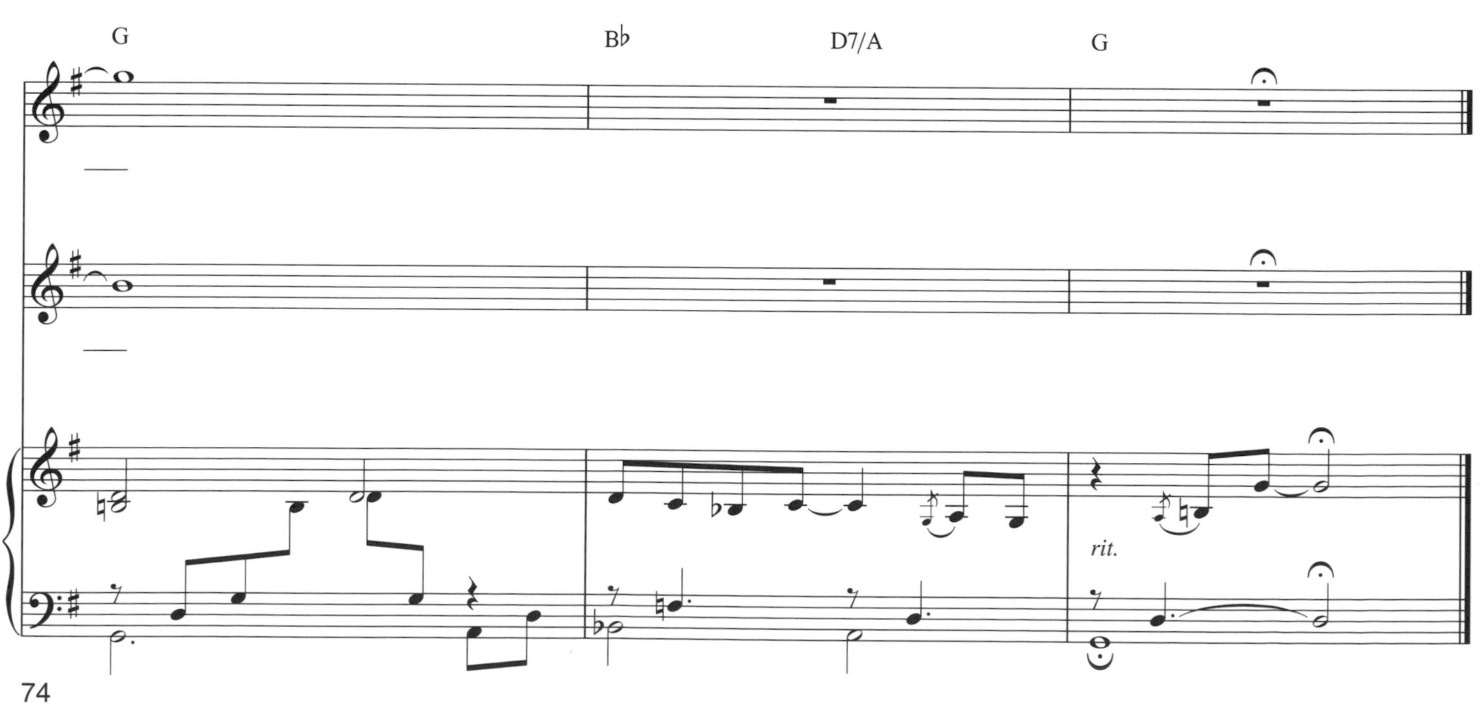
G
B♭
D7/A
G
rit.

May You Always

Words and Music by
Larry Markes and Dick Charles

A7
Dm7
A7
D7
G
for a smile be - comes you so.
May good for - tune
for a smile be - comes you so.
Ooh
B7
Em
G7
find your door - way, may the blue - bird sing your song.
C
C#o7
G/D
Bm
Em
A7
D9
D7♭9
G
May no trou - ble trav - el your way, may no wor - ry stay too long.
May no trou - ble trav - el your way, may no wor - ry stay too long.

G Em Am7 D7 G Em Am D7 E7
May your heart - aches be for - got - ten, may no tears be spilled. May
May your heart - aches be for - got - ten, may no tears be spilled. May
A F#m Bm7 E7 A6 A9sus4 Em7 A13
old ac - quain - tance be re - mem - bered, and your cup of
old ac - quain - tance be re - mem - bered, and your cup of
D#°/A Em A7 D7 G B7
kind - ness filled. And may you al - ways be a dream - er,
kind - ness filled. And may you al - ways be a dream - er,

1.
2.
Em G7 C C#° G/D G7 E7#5
may your wild - est dream come true. May you find some - one to love as
may your wild - est dream come true. May you find some - one to love as
A7 C/D D7 G G/D E7#5 E7 A7 A13
much as I love you. one to love as much as
much as I love you. one to love as much as
Am7 D7 G G+ G6
I love you.
I love you.

Oh, Promise Me
from ROBIN HOOD

Words by Clement Scott

Music by Reginald de Koven

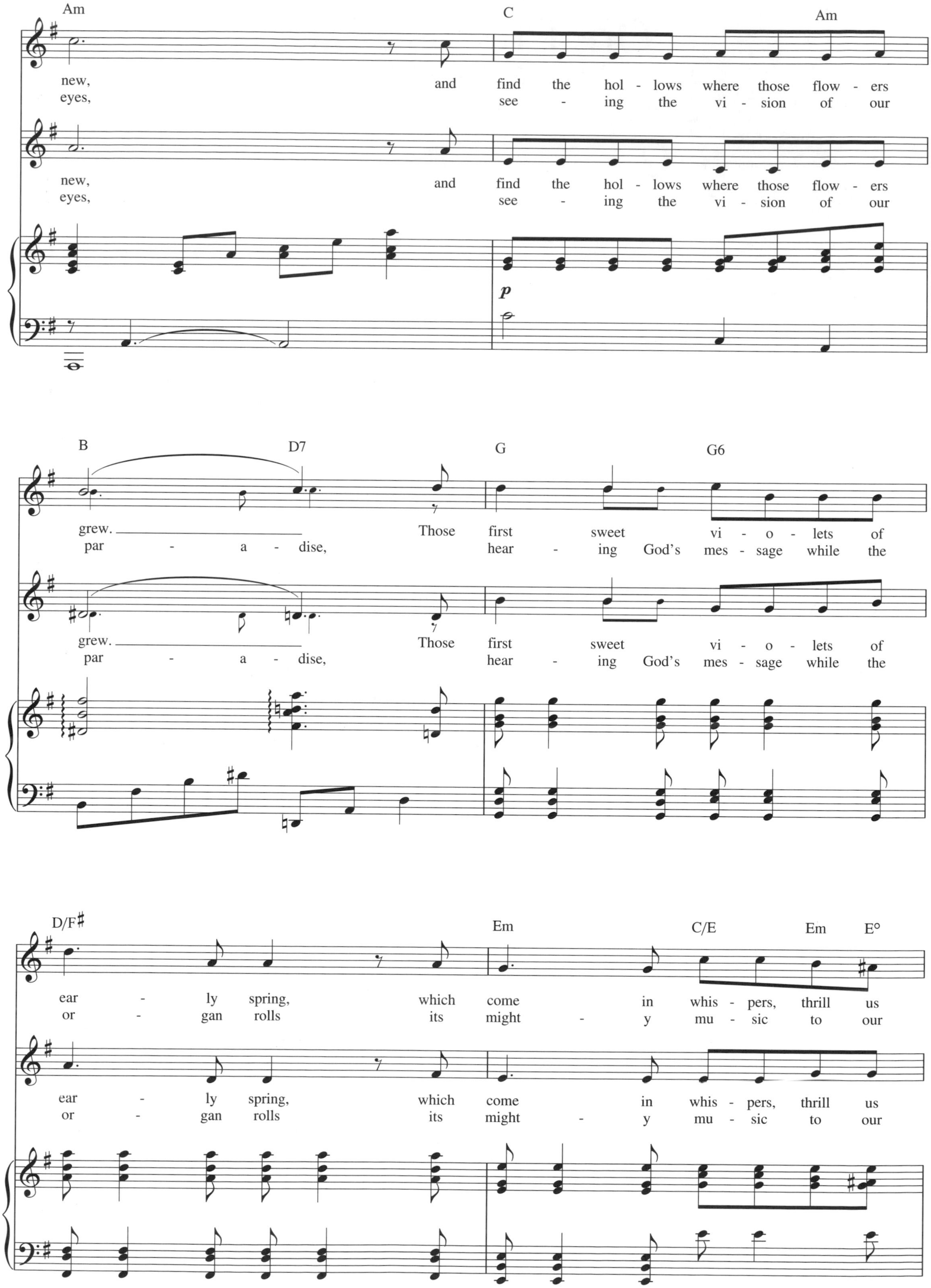

Am C Am

new, and find the hol - lows where those flow - ers
eyes, see - ing the vi - sion of our

new, and find the hol - lows where those flow - ers
eyes, see - ing the vi - sion of our

p

B D7 G G6

grew. Those first sweet vi - o - lets of
par - a - dise, hear - ing God's mes - sage while the

grew. Those first sweet vi - o - lets of
par - a - dise, hear - ing God's mes - sage while the

B/D♯ B C B
both, and sing of love un - speak - a - ble that
ver - y souls. No love less per - fect than a
both, and sing of love un - speak - a - ble that
ver - y souls. No love less per - fect than a
Em Cm6/E♭ E♭7
1.
G/D C/D G/D C/D D7
is to be; oh, prom - ise me, oh, prom - ise
life with thee; oh,
is to be; oh, prom - ise me, oh, prom - ise
life with thee; oh,
rit.
G
2.
G/D C/D G/D C/D D7 G
me. Oh, prom - ise me, oh, prom - ise me.
me. Oh, prom - ise me, oh, prom - ise me.
a tempo
rit.
Ped. * Ped. *

Panis Angelicus

(O Lord Most Holy)

By Cesar Franck

*Sing either English or Latin text.

O lov - ing Fa - ther, Thee would we be prais - ing al - ways.
dat pa - nis coe - li - cus fi - gu - ris ter - mi - num.
O lov - ing Fa - ther, Thee would we be prais - ing al - ways.
dat pa - nis coe - li - cus fi - gu - ris ter - mi - num.
Help us to know Thee, know Thee and
O res mi - ra - bi - lis, man - du - cat
Help us to know Thee, know Thee and
O res mi - ra - bi - lis, man - du - cat
love Thee. Fa - ther, Fa - ther, grant us Thy truth and
Do - mi - num, pau - per, pau - per, ser - vus et hu - mi-
love Thee. Fa - ther, Fa - ther, grant us Thy truth and
Do - mi - num, pau - per, pau - per, ser - vus et hu - mi -

grace. Fa - ther, Fa - ther, guide and de - fend
lis. Pau - per, pau - per, ser - vus et hu - mi-
grace. Fa - ther, Fa - ther, guide and de - fend
lis. Pau - per, pau - per, ser - vus et hu - mi -
us.
lis.
us.
lis.
Rule Thou our will - ful hearts; keep Thee our
Pa - nis an - ge - li - cus fit pa - nis
*Rule Thou our will - ful hearts;
Pa - nis an - ge - li - cus
mf

*May be sung an octave lower, if necessary (next 15 bars).

wan - d'ring thoughts. In all our sor - rows let us
ho - mi - num dat pa - nis coe - li - cus fi -
keep Thee our wan - d'ring thoughts. In all our
fit pa - nis ho - mi - num dat pa - nis

find our rest in Thee. Aid in temp - ta - tion's hour,
gu - ris ter - mi - num. O res mi - ra - bi - lis
sor - rows let us find our rest in Thee. Aid in temp -
coe - li - cus fi - gu - ris ter - mi - num. O res mi -

save through Thy might - y pow'r. Thine aid O
man - du - cat Do - mi - num, pau - per,
ta - tion's hour, save through Thy might - y pow'r.
ra - bi - lis man - du - cat Do - mi - num,

send us; hear us in mer - cy.
pau - per, ser - vus et hu - mi - lis.
Thine aid O hear us in mer - cy.
pau - per, ser - vus et hu - mi - lis.

Show us Thy fa - vor, so shall we live, and sing praise to
Pau - per, pau - per, ser - vus, ser - vus et hu - mi -
Show us Thy fa - vor, sing praise to
Pau - per, pau - per, et hu - mi -
rit. e dim.

Thee.
lis.
Thee.
lis.
mp
a tempo
rit.

Perhaps Love

Words and Music by
John Denver

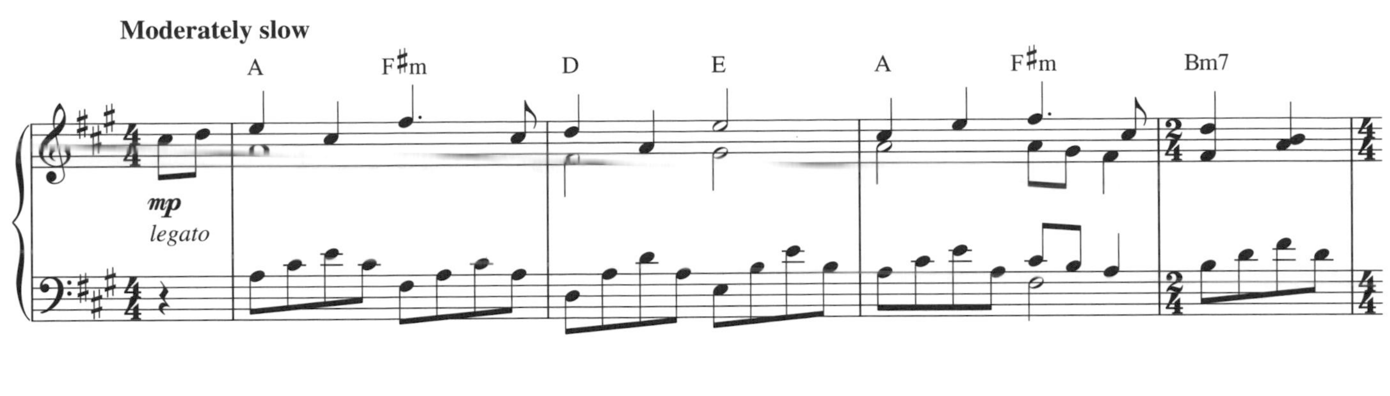

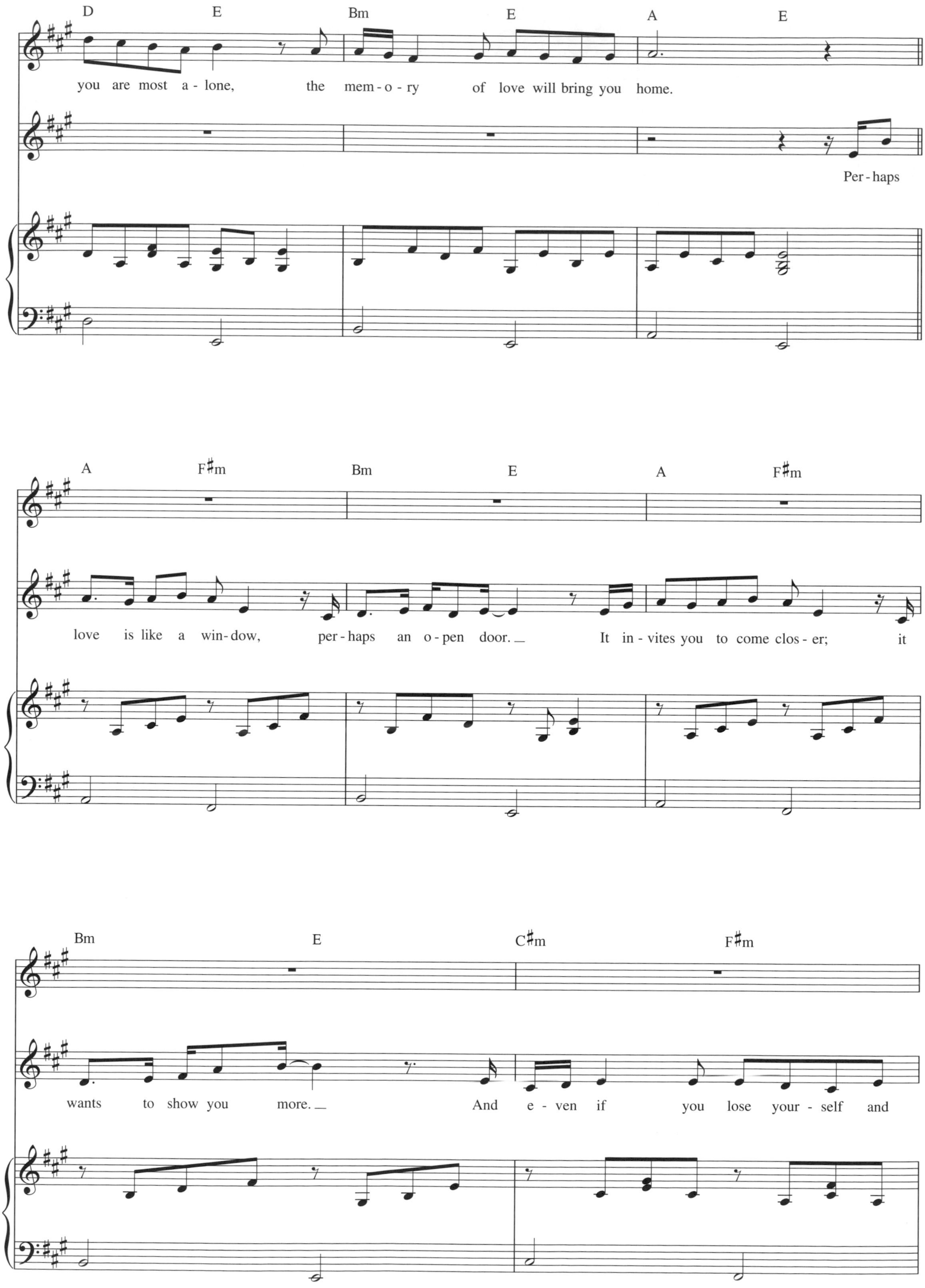

D E Bm E A E

you are most a - lone, the mem - o - ry of love will bring you home.

Per - haps

A F♯m Bm E A F♯m
love is like a win - dow, per - haps an o - pen door. It in - vites you to come clos - er; it

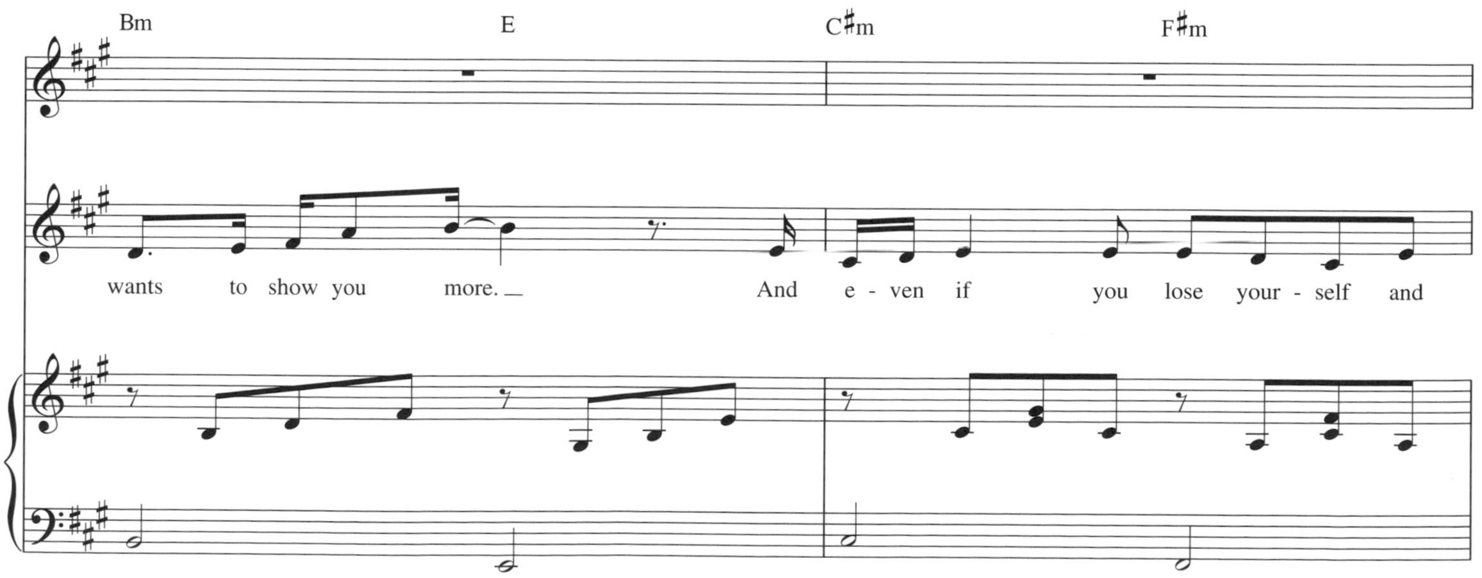
Bm E C♯m F♯m
wants to show you more. And e - ven if you lose your - self and

D
E
Bm
E
A
Oh,
don't know what to do, the mem-o-ry of love will see you through.
C♯m
F♯m
D
E
A
C♯m
F♯m
love to some is like a cloud, to some as strong as steel.
For some a way of liv-ing, for
D
E
A
C♯m
F♯m
And some say love is hold-ing on and
some a way to feel. And some say love is hold-ing on and

D E A C♯m F♯m Bm
some say let - ting go, and some say love is ev - 'ry - thing, and some say they don't
some say let - ting go.
rit.
E A F♯m
know. Full of
Per - haps love is like the o - cean, full of
a tempo
Bm E A F♯m
con - flict, full of pain, like a fi - re when it's cold out - side,
con - flict, full of pain, like a fi - re when it's cold out - side,

Bm E C♯m F♯m
thun - der when it rains. If I should live for - ev - er and
thun - der when it rains. If I should live for - ev - er and
D E Bm E
all my dreams come true, my mem - o - ries of love will be of
all my dreams come true, my mem - o - ries of love will be of
1. A 2. A F♯m D E A
you. Oh, you.
you. you.
rit.

Simple Gifts

Traditional Shaker Hymn

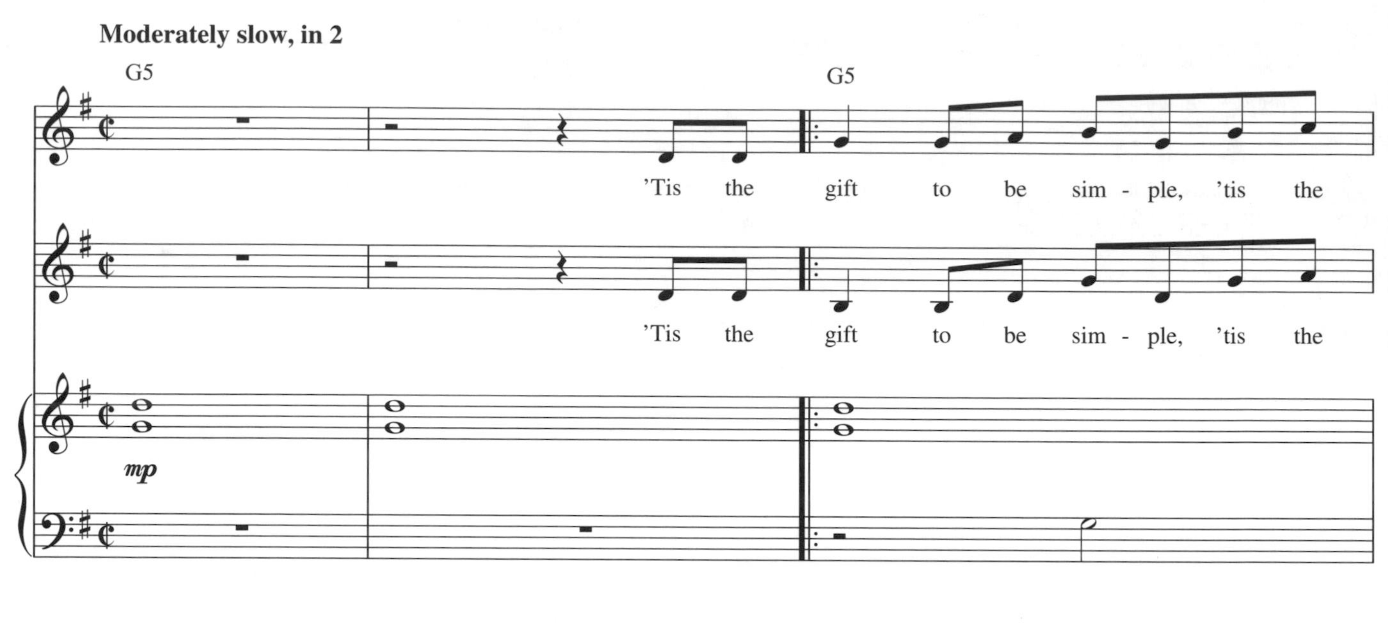

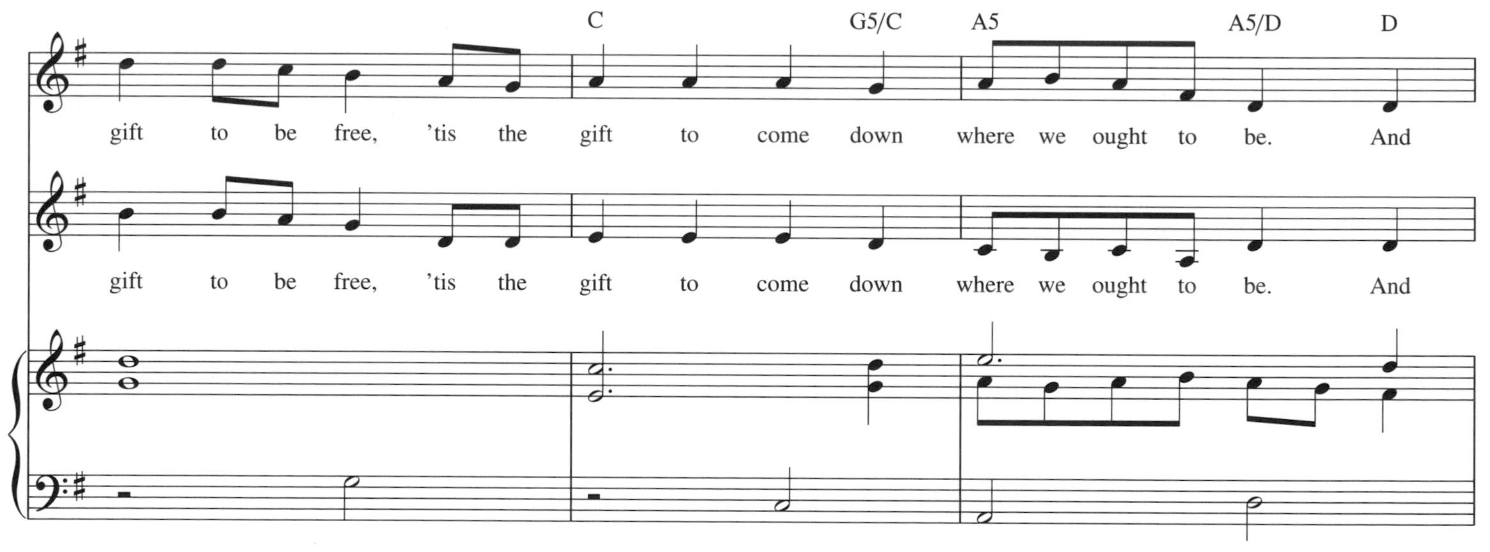

D5 G G5 G D/G Em D/E
love and de - light. When true sim - plic - i - ty is gained, to bow and to bend we
love and de - light. When true sim - plic - i - ty is gained, to bow and to bend we
L.H.
Am D5 N.C. C/E G/F♯ Em7
shan't be a - shamed. To turn, turn, will be our de - light till by
shan't be a - shamed. To turn, turn, will be our de - light till by
1. 2.
Am Bm7 Cmaj7 Bm/D C/E C/D G C/E C/D G
turn - ing, turn - ing, we come 'round right. 'Tis the come 'round right.
turn - ing, turn - ing, we come 'round right. 'Tis the come 'round right.
rit.

Sunrise, Sunset

from the Musical FIDDLER ON THE ROOF

Lyrics by Sheldon Harnick

Music by Jerry Bock

B♭m
G
G7
C7♯5
old - er. When did they?
see them, side be side.
Fm
C7
Fm
When did she get to be a beau - ty? When did he
Place the gold ring a - round her fin - ger. Share the sweet
When did she get to be a beau - ty? When did he
Place the gold ring a - round her fin - ger. Share the sweet
C7
Fm
F7
B♭m
F7
grow to be so tall? Was - n't it yes - ter - day when
wine and break the glass. Soon the full cir - cle will have
grow to be so tall? Was - n't it yes - ter - day when
wine and break the glass. Soon the full cir - cle will have

B♭m
G7
C
C7
C+
they
come
were
to
small?
pass.
they
come
were
to
small?
pass.

C7
Fm
C7
Fm
C7
Sun - rise,
sun - set,
sun - rise,
sun - set,
Sun - rise,
sun - set,
sun - rise,
sun - set,

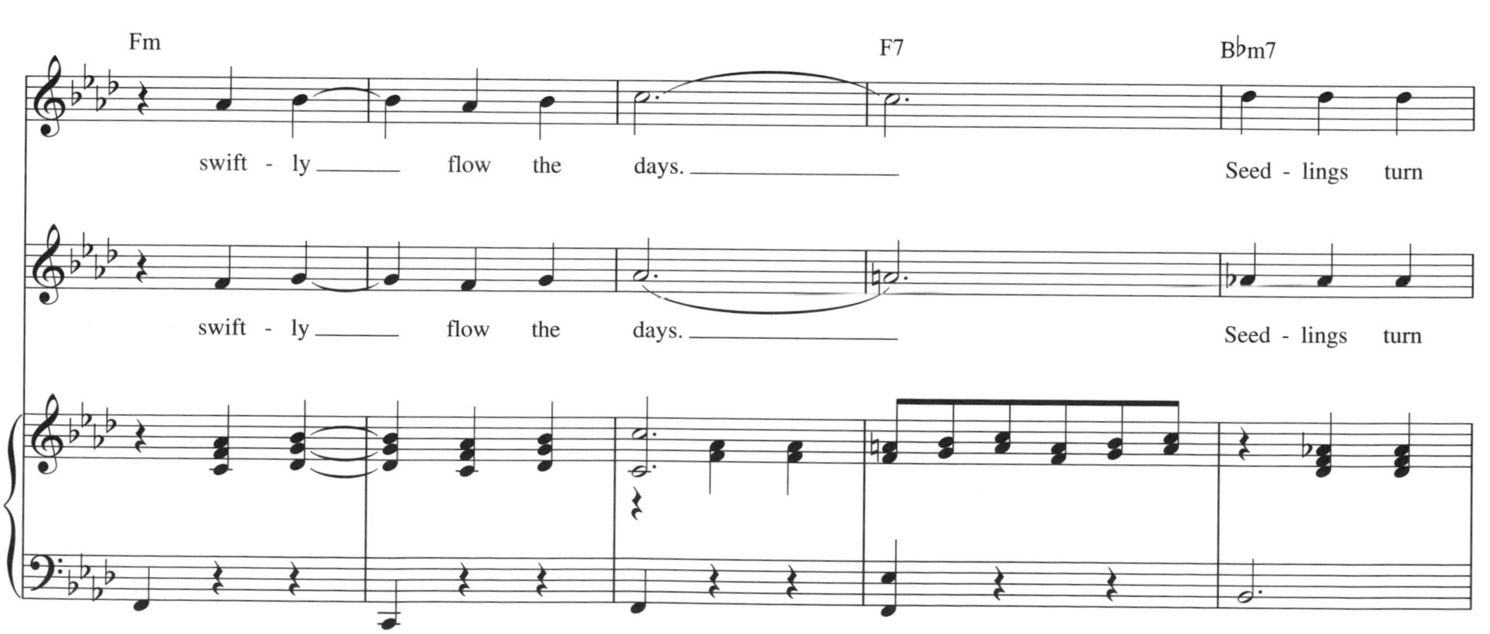
Fm
F7
B♭m7
swift - ly
flow the
days.
Seed - lings turn
swift - ly
flow the
days.
Seed - lings turn

E♭7
A♭maj7
A♭6
Gm7♭5
C7
o - ver night to sun - flow'rs, blos - som - ing e - ven as we
o - ver night to sun - flow'rs, blos - som - ing e - ven as we
Fm
Fm
C7
Fm
gaze. Sun - rise, sun - set, sun - rise,
gaze. Sun - rise, sun - set, sun - rise,
C7
Fm
F7
sun - set, swift - ly fly the years.
sun - set, swift - ly fly the years.

Gm7♭5
C7
Fm7
B♭9
Gm7♭5
One sea - son fol - low - ing an - oth - er, la - den with
One sea - son fol - low - ing an - oth - er, la - den with
1.
C7
Fm
hap - pi - ness and tears.
hap - pi - ness and tears.
2.
C7
Fm
hap - pi - ness and tears.
hap - pi - ness and tears.
rit.

Through the Years

Words and Music by
Steve Dorff and Marty Panzer

Cmaj7
D/C
Bm7
C/D
I
for an - y - one but you.
I
Gadd2
F#m7
B7
Em7
Dm7
G7
swear.
swear we've been through ev - 'ry - thing there is.
Can't i - mag - ine an - y - thing we've
Cmaj9
Gadd2/B
Am7
C/D
Through the
missed; can't i - mag - ine an - y - thing the two of us can't do. Through the

G
Emsus4 2
Em
Am7
C/D
D/C
years you've nev - er let me down; you've turned my life a -
years, through all the good and bad, I know how much we
mf
Bm7
Em7
round. The sweet - est days I've found I've found with you. Through the
had. I've al - ways been so glad to be with you. Through the
Bm7
E7
Am7
D
D/C
years I've nev - er been a - fraid; I've loved the life we've
years it's bet - ter ev - 'ry day; you've kissed my tears a -

Bm7 E7♭9 Cmaj9
made, and I'm so glad I've stayed right here with you
way. As long as it's o - kay, I'll stay with you
made, and I'm so glad I've stayed right here with you
way. As long as it's o - kay, I'll stay with you
To Coda
Am7 C/D Gadd2 Emsus4/2 Em Csus4/2 C C/D
through the years. I
through the
through the years.
through the
G F♯m7 B7 Em Dm7 G7
can't re - mem - ber what I used to do, who I trust - ed, who

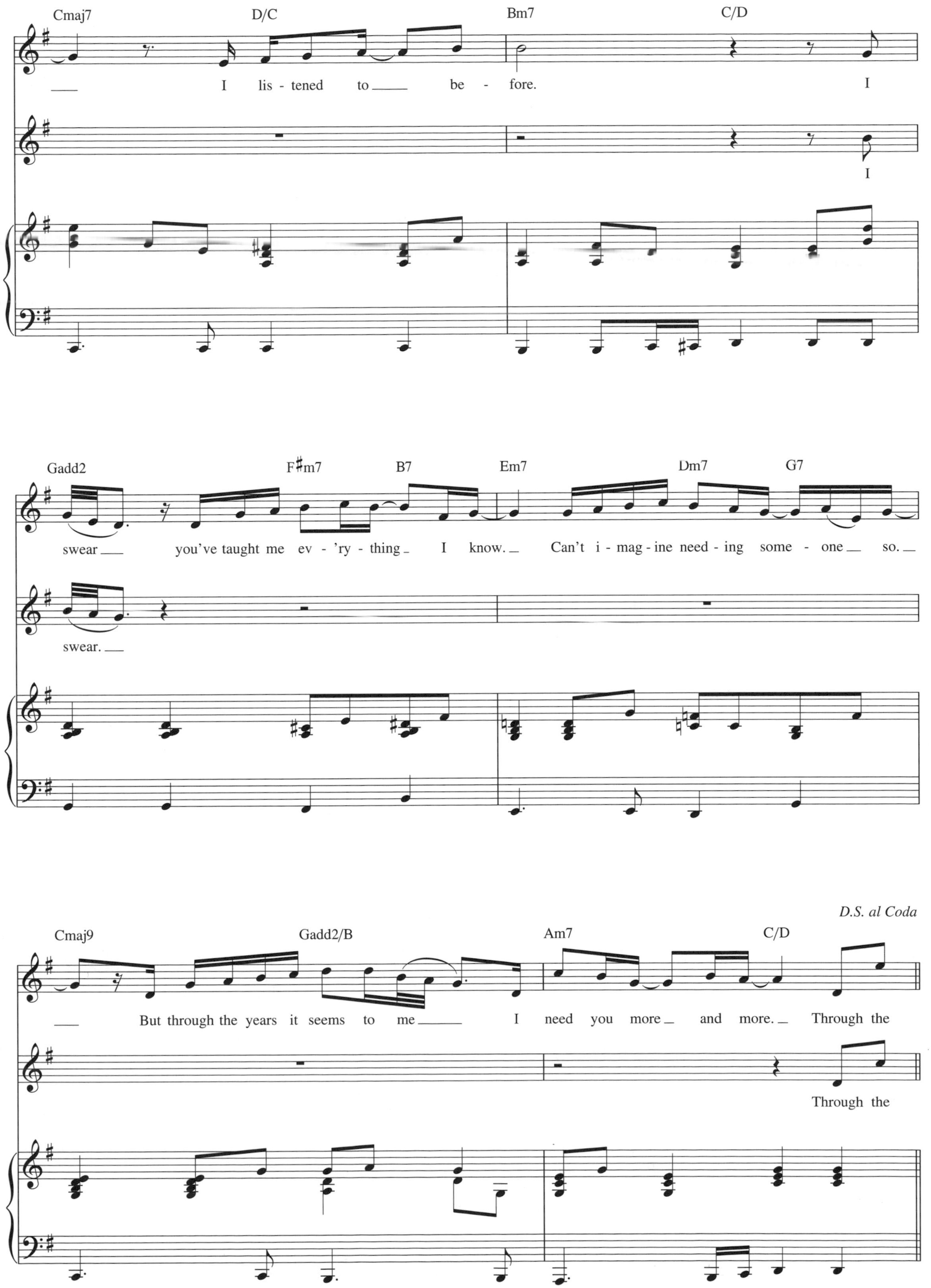

Cmaj7 D/C Bm7 C/D

I lis - tened to be - fore. I

I

Gadd2 F♯m7 B7 Em7 Dm7 G7

swear you've taught me ev - 'ry - thing I know. Can't i - mag - ine need - ing some - one so.

swear.

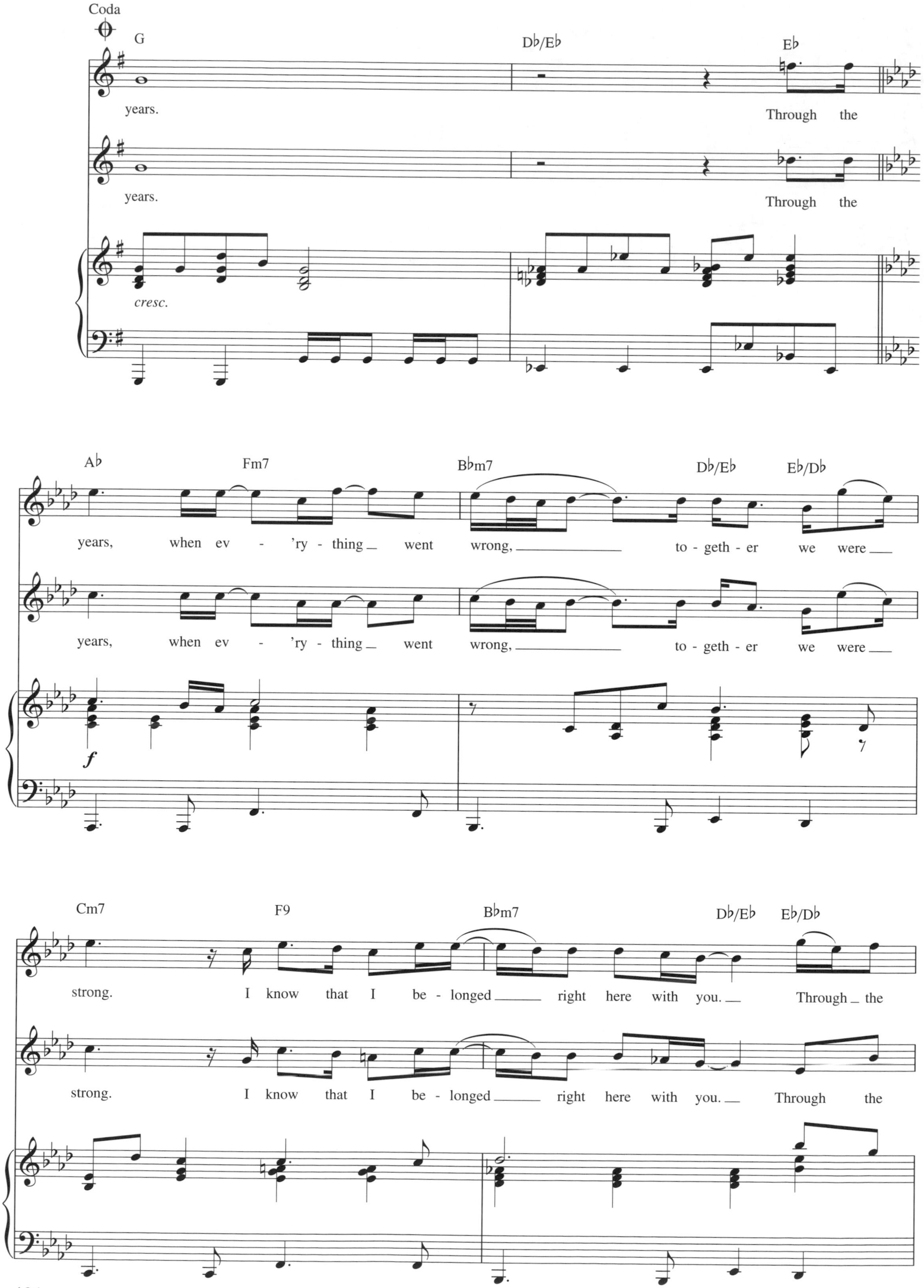

Coda
G
D♭/E♭
E♭
years. Through the
years. Through the
cresc.
A♭
Fm7
B♭m7
D♭/E♭
E♭/D♭
years, when ev - 'ry - thing went wrong, to - geth - er we were
years, when ev - 'ry - thing went wrong, to - geth - er we were
f
Cm7
F9
B♭m7
D♭/E♭
E♭/D♭
strong. I know that I be - longed right here with you. Through the
strong. I know that I be - longed right here with you. Through the

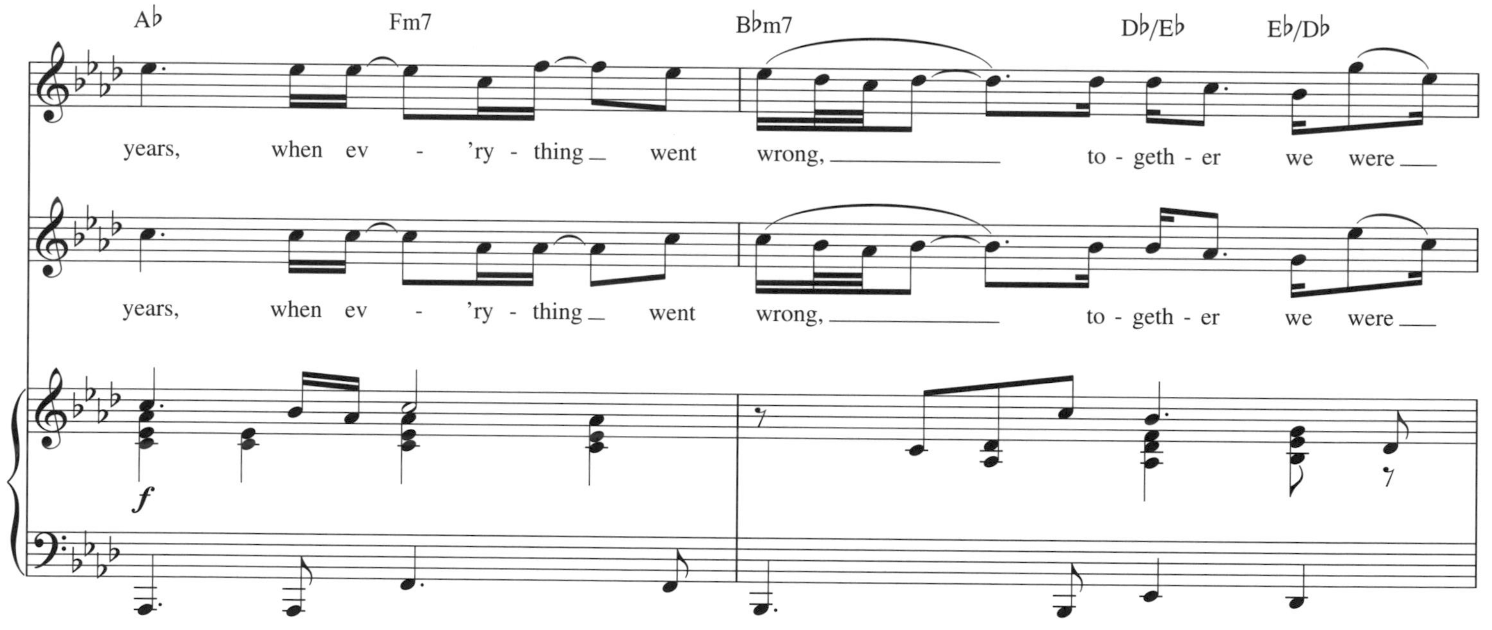

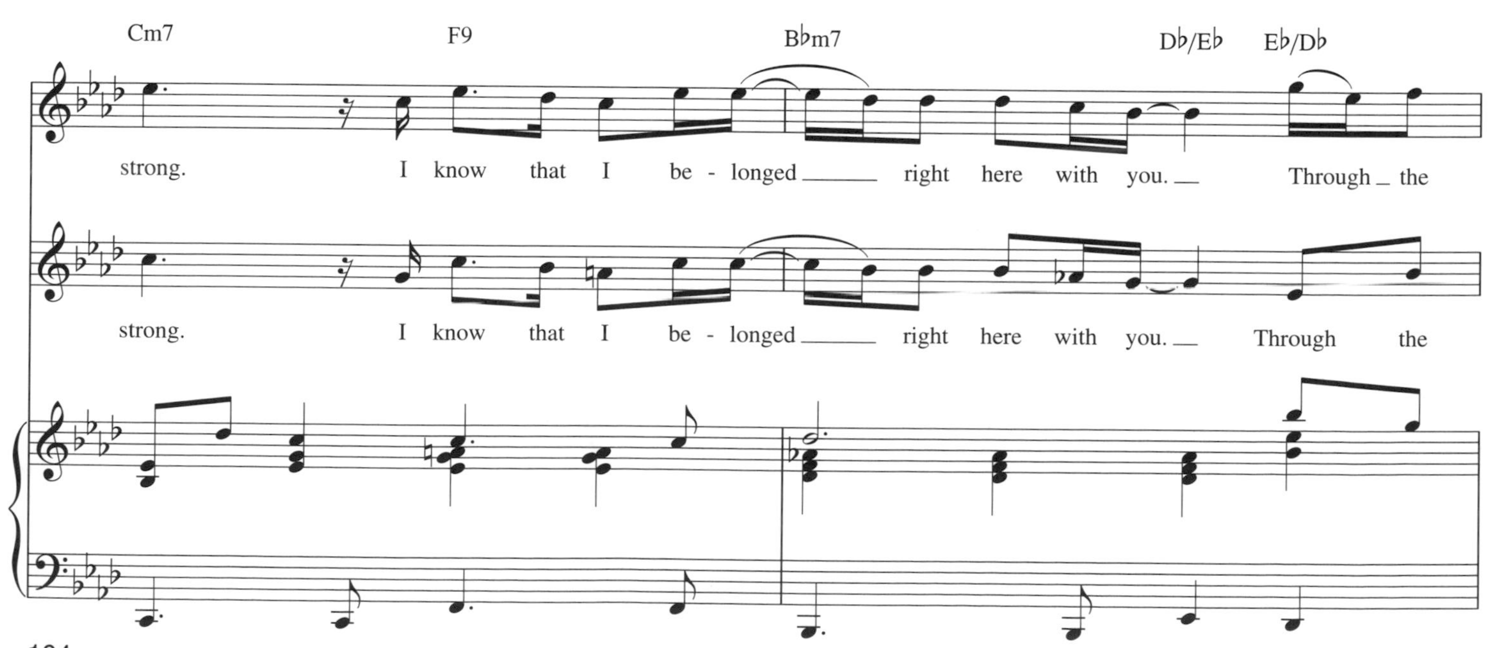

Cm7
F9
B♭m7
E♭9
E♭/D♭
years I nev - er had a doubt we'd al - ways work things
years I nev - er had a doubt we'd al - ways work things
Cm7
F9
D♭maj9
out. I've learned what love's a - bout by lov - ing
out. I've learned what love's a - bout by lov - ing
B♭m7
D♭/E♭
A♭
D♭maj7
A♭
you through the years.
you through the years.
rit.

We've Only Just Begun

Words and Music by
Roger Nichols and Paul Williams

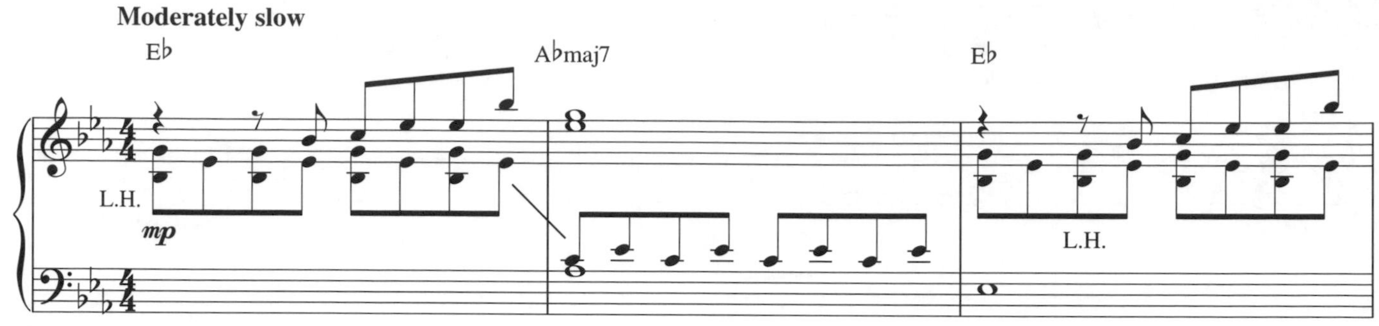

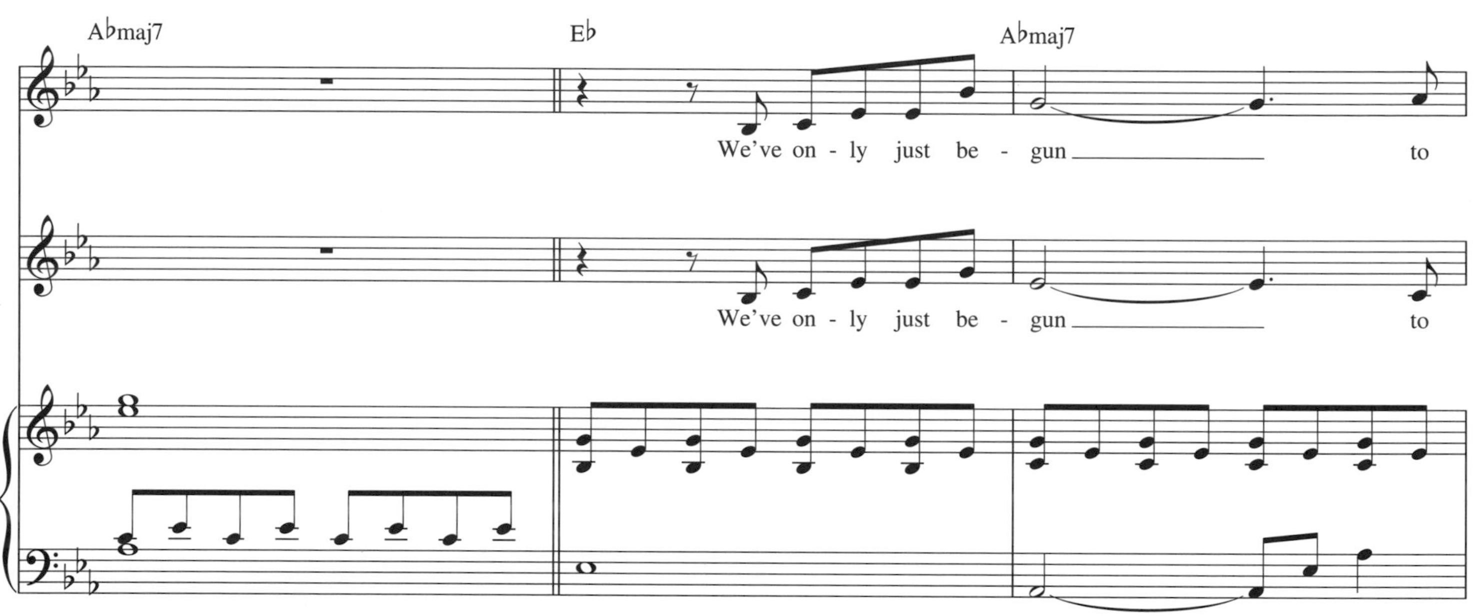

Cmadd2
Fm7
A♭/B♭
B♭
a kiss for luck and we're on our way.
a kiss for luck and we're on our way.
E♭
A♭maj7
Be - fore the ris - ing sun we
And when the eve - ning comes we
Be - fore the ris - ing sun we
And when the eve - ning comes we
(mp)
Gm7
Cmadd2
Fm7
fly; so man - y roads to choose;
smile; so much of life a - head;
fly; so man - y roads to choose;
smile; so much of life a - head;

To Coda
Cmadd2
Fm7
we start out walk - ing and learn to run.
we'll find a place where there's room to grow.
we start out walk - ing and learn to run.
we'll find a place where there's room to grow.
B♭
E♭
A♭maj7
E♭
A♭maj7
B♭
And yes, we've just be - gun.
And yes, we've just be - gun.
cresc.
mf
C
Fmaj7
C
Fmaj7
Shar - ing ho - ri - zons that are new to us,
Shar - ing ho - ri - zons that are new to us,

C
Fmaj7
C
Fmaj7
watch - ing the signs a - long the way.
watch - ing the signs a - long the way.

Emaj7
Amaj7
Emaj7
Amaj7
Talk - ing it o - ver, just the two of us,
Talk - ing it o - ver, just the two of us,

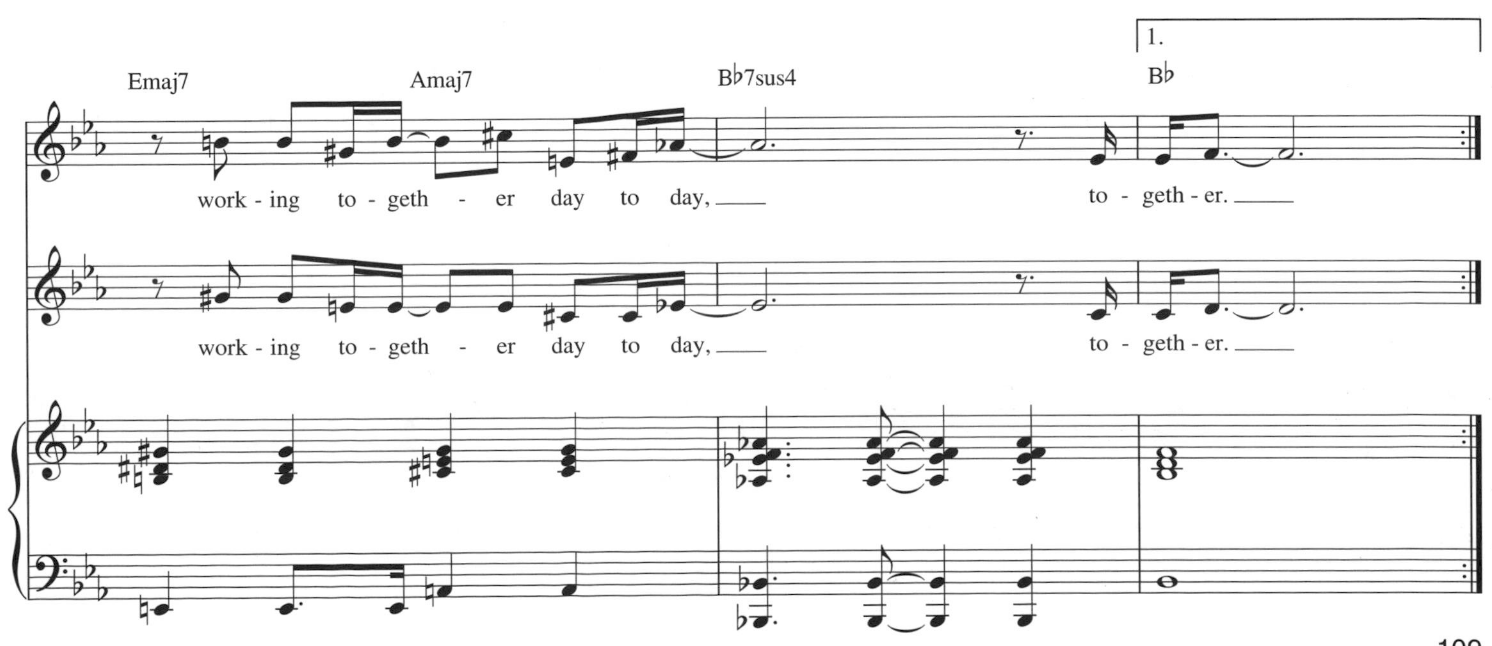
1.
Emaj7
Amaj7
B♭7sus4
B♭
work - ing to - geth - er day to day, to - geth - er.
work - ing to - geth - er day to day, to - geth - er.

2.
B♭
D.S. (lyric 2) al Coda
geth - er, to - geth - er.
geth - er, to - geth - er.
Coda
B♭
And yes, we've just be -
And yes, we've just be -

E♭
A♭maj7
gun.
gun.
L.H.

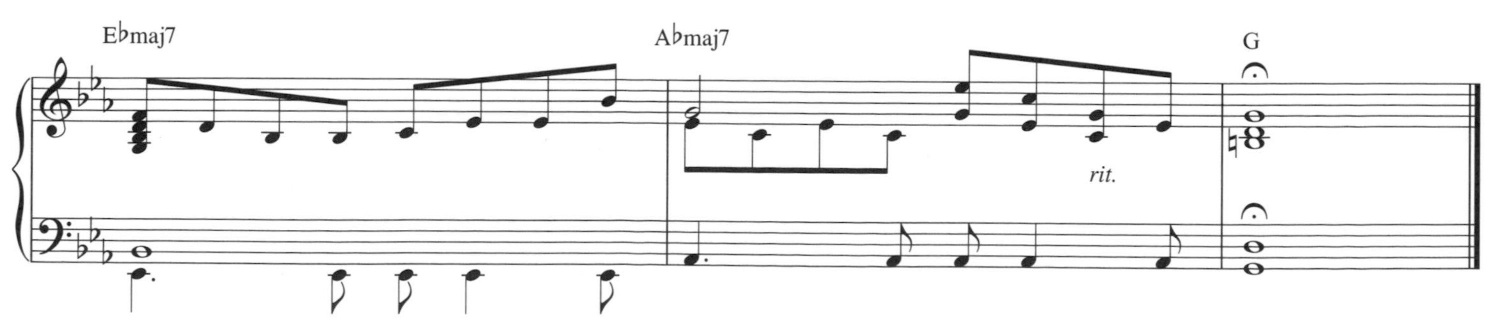
E♭maj7
A♭maj7
G
rit.

When I Fall in Love

from ONE MINUTE TO ZERO

Words by Edward Heyman

Music by Victor Young

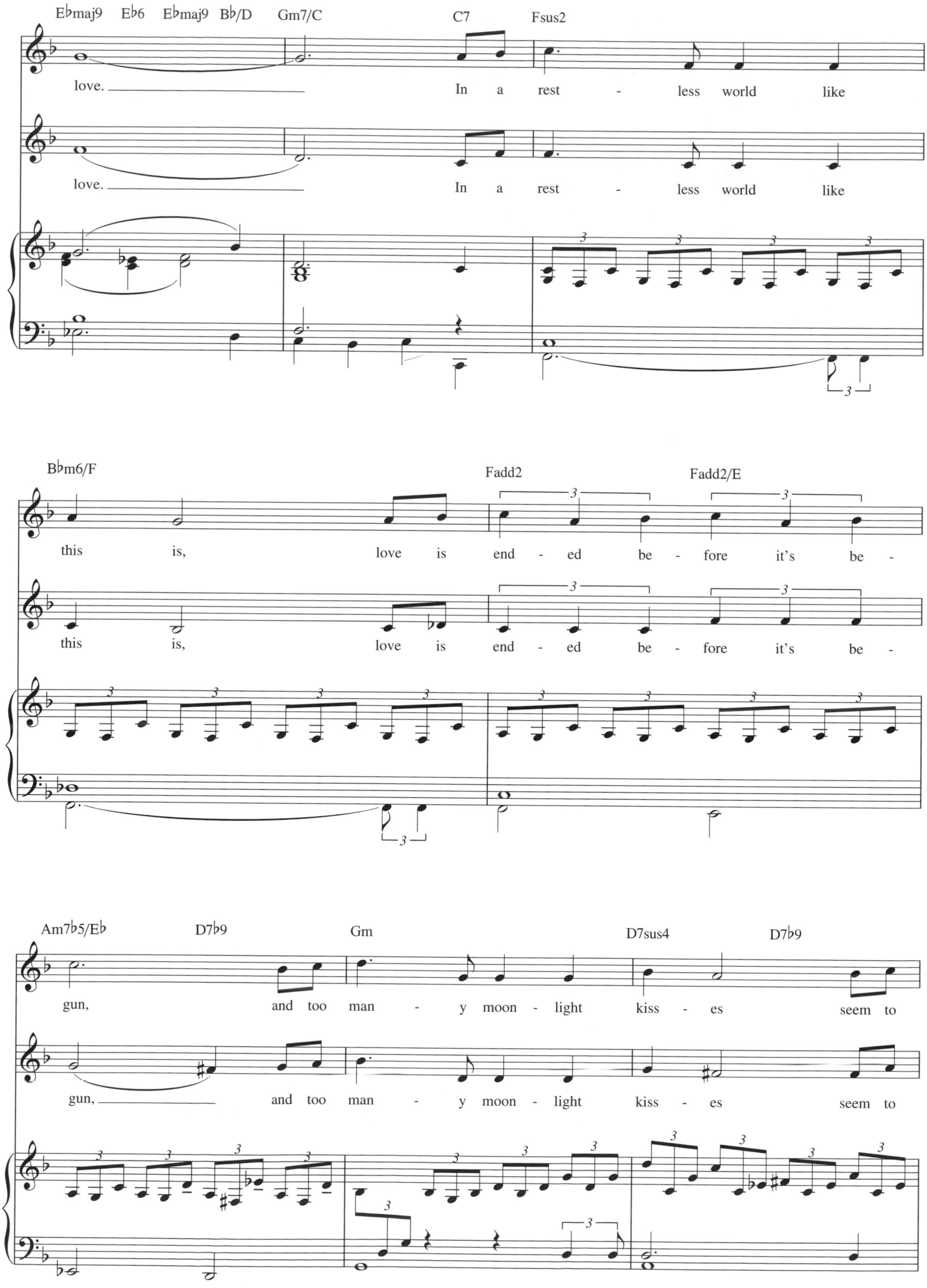

E♭maj9 E♭6 E♭maj9 B♭/D Gm7/C C7 Fsus2
love. In a rest - less world like
love. In a rest - less world like
B♭m6/F Fadd2 Fadd2/E
this is, love is end - ed be - fore it's be -
this is, love is end - ed be - fore it's be -
Am7♭5/E♭ D7♭9 Gm D7sus4 D7♭9
gun, and too man - y moon - light kiss - es seem to
gun, and too man - y moon - light kiss - es seem to

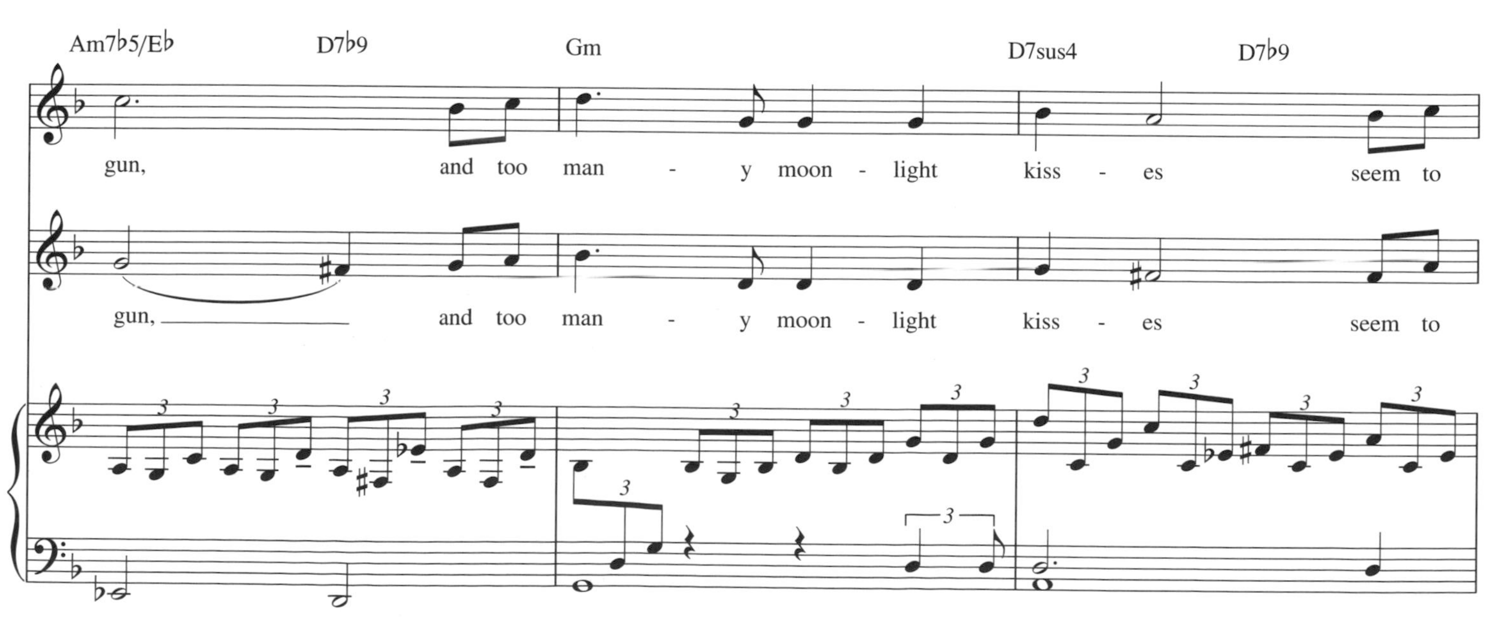

Gm
Gm/F♯
Gm/F
Fsus2
C/E
C
F
B♭sus2/D
cool in the warmth of the sun.
When I give my
cool in the warmth of the sun.
When I give my
rit.
a tempo
F/C
B♭sus2
F/A
B♭/D
F/C
B♭6
Gm
C7
heart, it will be com - plete - ly,
heart, it will be com - plete - ly,
F
B♭add2
Fmaj7/A
Dm9
Dm7
G
or I'll nev - er give my heart.
or I'll nev - er give my heart.

C7sus4 C7 C/B♭ F/A F B♭
And the mo - ment I can feel that you
And the mo - ment I can feel that you
Am7 D7 B♭m/D♭ E♭m/D♭ B♭m/D♭ E♭m/D♭ Fadd2/C B♭add2/D
feel that way too is when I fall in
feel that way too is when I fall in
Gm7 C F
love with you.
love with you.
rit.
a tempo
pp

Your Song

Words and Music by
Elton John and Bernie Taupin

E♭/B♭
B♭
G/B
Cmadd2
don't _ have much mon - ey ________ but, boy, if ___ I did,
But the sun's _ been quite kind ________ while I wrote this song.
don't _ have much mon - ey ________ but, _ boy, if ___ I did, ____
But the sun's _ been quite kind ________ while I wrote this song. ____
E♭
Fm7
A♭
I'd buy ___ a big house where _ we both ___ could
It's for peo - ple like you that ___ keep it ____ turned
I'd buy ___ a big house where ______ we both ___ could
It's for peo - ple like you that ______ keep it ____ turned
B♭
B♭sus4
B♭
E♭
A♭maj7
live. If I was a sculp - tor,
on. So ex - cuse me for - get - ting,
live. If I was a sculp - tor,
on. So ex - cuse me for - get - ting,

B♭/D
Gm
Cmadd2
Cm/B♭
but then a - gain, no, or a man who makes po - tions in a
but these things I do. You see, I've for - got - ten if they're
Am7♭5
A♭6
E♭/B♭
B♭
trav - el - ing show, I know it's not much, but it's the best
green or they're blue. An - y - way, the thing is, what I real - ly
G/B
Cmadd2
E♭
Fm7
I can do. My gift is my song and
mean: Yours are the sweet - est eyes

A♭
E♭
A♭/E♭
E♭
this one's for you.
I've ev - er seen.
this one's for you.
I've ev - er seen.
*cresc.
*1st time only
B♭/D
Cm
Fm
A♭
And you can tell ev - 'ry - bod - y this is your song.
And you can tell ev - 'ry - bod - y this is your song.
mf
B♭/D
Cm
Fm
A♭
It may be quite sim - ple but now that it's done,

Cm
Cm/B♭
Am7♭5
I hope you don't mind, I hope you don't mind that I put down in
I hope you don't mind, I hope you don't mind that I put down in
A♭6
E♭/G
A♭6
words how won - der - ful life is while you're in the world.
words how won - der - ful life is while you're in the world.
B♭
B♭sus4
B♭
1.
E♭
A♭/E♭
B♭/E♭
A♭/E♭
mp

2.
Cm
Cm/B♭
Cm/A
I hope you don't mind, I hope you don't mind that I put down in
I hope you don't mind, I hope you don't mind that I put down in
A♭6
E♭/G
A♭6
words how won - der - ful life is while you're in the world.
words how won - der - ful life is while you're in the world.
E♭
A♭/E♭
B♭/E♭
A♭/E♭
E♭